July 2002.
Happy Birthday Isabel!
from
Annemies xx

D1643685

A Magna Colour Guide

Indoor Plants

A Magna Colour Guide

Indoor Plants

by Jan Přibyl

Illustrations
by Zdeněk Berger

MAGNA
BOOKS

Text by Jan Přibyl
Illustrations by Zdeněk Berger
Translated by Eva Klimentová
Graphic design by František Prokeš

This edition published 1995 by
Magna Books
Magna Road, Wigston,
Leicester LE18 4ZH,
and produced in co-operation with
Arcturus Publishing Limited

ISBN 1 85422 839 0
Printed in Slovakia by Neografia, Martin
3/15/20/51-02

CONTENTS

GROWING PLANTS INDOORS

The indoor environment has its own microclimate which differs markedly from those in our house plants' natural habitats, which best suit their healthy growth and development. But in this special microclimate they depend on the same vital factors — light, temperature, water, air and nutrients.

All these factors are interdependent and it is our task to keep them in balance. Undesirably high temperatures in summer, for instance, can be reduced by more frequent watering and good air circulation. Plants exposed to low temperatures on the other hand need little moisture. But this approach has only a temporary effect. To succeed at growing house plants one must bear in mind the rule that each vital factor — light, water, nutrients and so on — is indispensable. So if any of these factors is deficient it cannot be made up for by more of one of the others.

Particular attention should be given to light and temperature when considering indoor conditions. Also take the level of humidity, and in certain circumstances the amount and quality of the air, into account. The supply of water and nutrients can be regulated quite easily, so they do not have such a significant effect on the quality of the plant's environment.

Light

Light energy is used by all green, chlorophyll-containing plants to manufacture organic substances by means of the process known as photosynthesis. The level of photosynthesis generally depends on the intensity of the light, so with increased light intensity, the plant's development and growth will tend to be more rapid. But in practice each genus, species and sometimes even cultivar has its own light requirement. This is influenced by the age of the plant as well as by the quality of other vital factors.

Plants can be divided into two groups according to their light requirements:
1. Light-loving plants, which tolerate or require direct sunlight. They are grown without shading near a window all year round.
2. Shade-loving plants, which tolerate only a moderate intensity of light. A higher intensity can harm them, so they must not be exposed to direct sunlight. They should be grown in more or less shaded places except in November, December and the first half of January, when light is weak.

Besides the intensity of light, the number of hours of daylight plays an important role in the development of the plant. In our conditions, daylight hours are long in summer and short in winter. The duration of exposure to light has a direct influence on the rate of photosynthesis and in some plants also stimulates the change from vegetative growth to the reproductive phase. So plants can be further categorised according to the time of flower initiation. Short-day plants flower in short spring and autumn days, e.g. *Begonia* Elatior hybrids, chrysanthemum and poinsettia. Long-day plants flower in summer, for example urn plant and tuberous begonia. But many plants don't respond to daylength and can develop flowers at any season of the year.

Temperature

Increasing temperature has a stimulating effect on both photosynthesis and respiration, a fall in temperature has the opposite effect. Always consider the effects of temperature on the development and growth of the plant along with the influence of other factors, particularly light and humidity. Temperature requirements change together with the varying light intensity over the course of the year and during the day. The more intense the light, the higher the temperature should be and vice versa. This means in practice that in an air-conditioned flat where the temperature is fairly constant, conditions are far from ideal for photosynthesis.

To grow successfully a plant must have a particular range of temperatures. The ideal range is termed the optimum temperature, which gradually changes during the plant's life. In the pictorial section of this book the reader will find a note of the most desirable temperature for each species in winter when light is at its lowest intensity.

Higher temperatures are desirable for the reproduction of plants than for normal growth. The geographic origin of the plants is a most influential factor. The optimum temperature for seed-sowing and germination varies from $16-25$ °C ($60-78$ °F). To reproduce house plants vegetatively from cuttings or by division, temperatures can range from 18 to 26 °C ($64-80$ °F). Only a few cold-loving plants will reproduce at lower temperatures.

Young plants need $3-5$ °C ($5-9$ °F) more warmth than mature ones. Higher temperatures are also desirable while plants are in flower.

The temperature of the compost has a direct influence on the uptake of nutrients, and should promote the steady growth of the plant. It can often be the same as the air temperature, particularly for plants of the temperate zone, but the compost for tropical and sub-tropical plants should be $2-4$ °C ($3.5-7$ °F) warmer than the surrounding air.

Day and night temperatures should not be the same. House plants are generally grown with higher day than night temperatures. The higher the intensity of daylight, the greater should be the difference between day and night temperatures. A good general rule is that the night temperature during the winter should be $2-4$ °C ($3.5-7$ °F) lower than the optimum day temperature.

House plants can be divided into four main groups according to their temperature requirements:

1. Species grown in a winter temperature higher than 21 °C (70 °F). These rather demanding plants are natives of the tropical rain forests. The average temperature should not fall below 18 °C (64 °F). They also require rather high air humidity (70% or more), so they should be grown in glass plant cases, flower windows or winter gardens.

2. Species that tolerate temperatures from 18 to 20 °C (64—68 °F) in winter and a humidity of less than 50%. They can tolerate wide temperature fluctuations in summer. These plants are natives of the deserts, sub-tropical forests and wooded steppes. They generally do well in centrally heated flats.

3. Species grown in winter at temperatures from 12 to 17 °C (54—63 °F). These are native to warm humid zones with no dry season. Various deciduous plants and evergreens of the laurel family belong to this group and are suitable even for rooms without central heating.

4. Species that winter at 5—7 °C (41—45 °F) come from temperate areas. Most of these are dormant in winter. Plants happy in cold conditions are suitable for decorating unheated halls and corridors, provided the temperature doesn't fall below freezing.

Water and Humidity

A plant's light and temperature requirements depend on its geographical origin, which also determines its requirements for humidity — the moisture in the atmosphere and in the compost in which it is growing. Humidity must be considered independently, for a lack of atmospheric moisture cannot be made up for by more frequent watering, or vice versa. Humidity requirements vary with the time of year and even with the time of day in some species.

The humidity of the air is one of the most important factors in growing house plants successfully. It varies widely as the temperature changes. When the temperature rises the humidity of the air falls continuously, which has a negative effect, especially in centrally heated rooms during the winter. It causes increased evaporation from the aerial parts of the plant, as well as limiting growth and producing such physiological troubles as falling and curling leaves, shrivelling blossoms and falling fruits.

The moisture content of the compost is regulated by the frequency of watering and the amount of water given to the plant. The water should be clean and low in minerals. Rainwater can be used in areas where it is not polluted with industrial smog. Elsewhere, the gardener will have to be content with tap water. The water should not be too hard. The hardness of water is expressed as the volume of lime it contains. Hard water should be boiled before use.

Never water plants with water that contains chlorine. Fat, mineral oils, cleaning agents, detergents and phenols are also harmful to plants.

Air

Apart from the oxygen received in adequate amounts from the air in normal conditions by aerial organs, the oxygen in the compost is vital to the life of the plant. A lack of oxygen in the soil will seriously damage its root system. So when mixing composts, be sure to add ingredients such as peat or perlite to keep the compost open and well aerated.

Beware of harmful gases that result from the combustion of certain substances. Sulphur dioxide and flue gases are the most dangerous. Gas, even in very low concentrations causes physiological disorders in plants. The air should also be reasonably free from dust particles, as dust hinders the plants' respiration and photosynthesis and the evaporation of water.

Nutrition

A plant's sensitivity to the supply of nutrients varies with the species, its age and the time of year. A shortage of nutrients will result in abnormal growth and poor flowering, but an excess can also be harmful. The level of salts in the soil solution (the liquid part of the soil) is increased, the plant's vitality is depressed and the aerial growth and roots deteriorate. An excessively high concentration of nutrients can even kill the plant.

Indoor plants fall into three categories as regards their nutrient requirements and their sensitivity to the concentration of salts in the soil:

1) Plants with low demands for nutrients and high sensitivity to the concentration of the soil solution, e.g. flamingo flower, rose heath, orchids and flaming sword.

2) Plants with moderate demands for food and medium sensitivity to the concentration of the soil solution. These include the urn plant, zebra plant, *Cyclamen persicum* and gloxinia.

3) Plants with high nutritional demands and low sensitivity to the concentration of the soil solution are e.g. *Asparagus densiflorus,* poinsettia and *Hydrangea macrophylla.* Young plants generally require a lower concentration of nutrients than mature plants.

For supplementary feeding, give liquid, concentrated, compound fertilisers containing only a very low volume of ballast substances. Most people use proprietary liquid house plant fertilisers as they form a convenient means of feeding plants.

Soil and Containers

Its roots play an important part in a plant's life. It receives water, air and nutrients from the soil solution through its roots, which is why it is essential for the roots to develop properly and remain in perfect health. Their growth and development depend largely on the properties of the compost, which should suit the needs of the plant.

When preparing compost for house plants, we should bear in mind that its physical properties, particularly its texture, air content and water capacity, should be as close as possible to those in the plant's natural habitat. Compost mixtures for house plants should therefore be formed of soil (loam), usually with the addition of river sand, perlite, vermiculite, sphagnum, peat, chopped bark or crushed brick. The mixture of ingredients can be varied according to the needs of the plant. A proprietary base fertiliser should be added to a compost mix, according to maker's instructions.

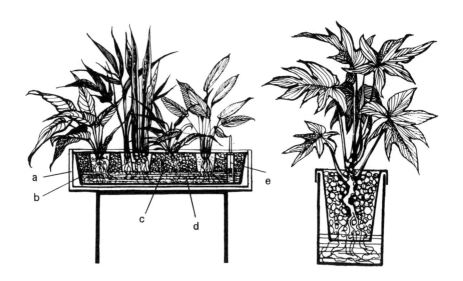

Hydroponics, or soilless culture, is a special way of growing plants. They receive all their food from a nutrient solution, usually prepared by dissolving a compound liquid fertiliser in water. The fertiliser contains the necessary major trace elements. A chemically inert medium (gravel or granules of some kind) is used instead of soil to help build a healthy root system. Plants are potted in unglazed ceramic or plastic pots (1). Several plants can be grouped in a hydroponic table (2): a) wooden container, b) plastic insert, c) sterile medium, d) nutrient solution, e) water gauge.

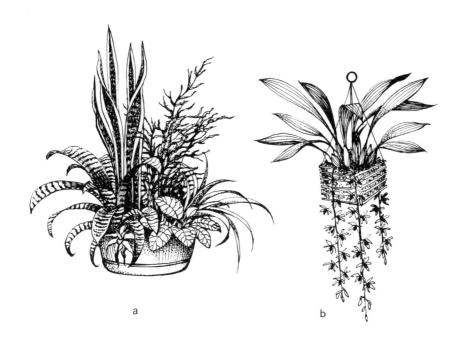

a   b

When grouping plants in large ceramic bowls (a), be careful to put together only those with similar requirements. Grouping upright and creeping plants with leaves of different shapes and sizes creates the most attractive effect. Bromeliads and epiphytic orchids can be potted in wooden baskets (b).

reaction, expressed on the pH scale. Strongly acid soils have a reaction lower than pH 4.5, acid soils have a pH from 4.5. to 5.4, weak acid soils from pH 5.5. to 6.5, and neutral with pH 7.0. The pH reaction can be easily measured with a simple test kit, available at garden centres. Large deviations from the optimum (usually considered 6.5) can damage roots or reduce the plants' ability to absorb and dissolve key nutrients. It is quite easy to make the reaction more alkaline. Add 1.5 g ($\frac{1}{2}$ oz) of ground limestone to 1 litre (0.26 gal) of soil to increase the pH by one degree. It is much more difficult however to lower the pH value of a soil. With alkaline or lime soils, increasing the proportion of strongly acid bog peat serves the purpose.

We can use the ready-mixed composts sold at garden centres for repotting, rather than mix our own. Light peat-based mixtures can be used wherever they suit the needs of the plant to be grown in them. Some plants prefer a soil (loam) based compost, such as John Innes potting compost No. 1 or 2.

Plants can also be grown in a nutrient solution. This is known as soilless culture or hydroponics.

House plants are generally grown in plastic flower pots or occasionally still in pots made of fired clay. Being porous, they let through a certain amount of water and air, so the soil dries out rather rapidly. The plants therefore require more frequent watering.

Plastic pots, being airproof and watertight, prevent the soil from drying out rapidly. These pots are lighter in weight, so they are suitable for the less vigorous plants. Large plants tend to be rather unstable if potted in plastic containers.

Cast pots or big bowls of glazed ceramic are not only very practical for growing indoor plants, but are valued for their decorative appearance. Their weight could cause problems though. Plastic bowls and larger containers imitate pottery in shape and colour and are easy to handle, light and durable. Wooden containers are suitable for big palms and wood-species grown on a balcony or terrace in summer. They are rather expensive, yet have a limited life. Orchids can be grown in special baskets made of hardwood laths or plastic.

Propagation

House plant enthusiasts can propagate many different kinds indoors. A propagator is a must for most of them. This is a closed glass or plastic covered box with regulated temperature and ventilation. A propagator should be stood in a light place but shaded when necessary.

Plants can be increased in two ways:
1. By sexual reproduction, that is from seeds or spores.
2. Vegetatively, by using a shoot, leaf or other part of the mother plant. This is the more common method used with house plants.

Seeds should be sown in a pot or small pan, filled with soft, light, permeable soil with a little fertiliser. A mixture of equal parts old leafmould, peat and sand, or of peat and sand, will do. This seed-sowing compost should be free from weed seeds and pest and disease organisms. Pure perlite has proved successful in practice too. Or use John Innes seed compost.

Sowing time varies with the kind of plant and the seed's capacity to germinate. February to April is the most favourable time for sowing. The sowing technique depends on the size of the seed. Small seeds and spores should be scattered thinly on the surface of the compost, larger ones can be covered with a thin layer of soil. Some species, such as bromeliads, germinate if exposed to light, while others, such as primulas do so only in the dark.

Moisten the sown seeds with a gentle spray of water. Stand the

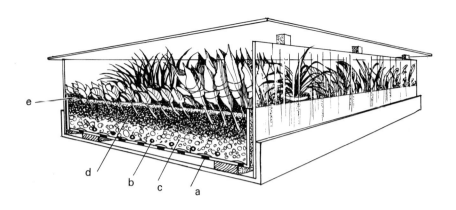

Propagator: a) drainage holes, b) electric heating cable, c) layer of drainage material, d) rooting medium e) thin layer of sand.

pots in a bowl of water to soak it up and moisten the compost from below.

Seeds germinate at different temperatures and humidity according to the species. Containers should be covered with glass or plastic sheet and shaded with paper if necessary. Transplant the seedlings in good time so the young plants have enough space to grow.

Only healthy, well-developed parts of mother plants are suitable for vegetative reproduction. All the plant's good qualities are then transmitted to the next generation. Propagation by cuttings is the most commonly used method. These may be stem cuttings from the tip or other parts of the stem, or leaf or root cuttings.

Cuttings should be sufficiently mature, as excessively soft growth quickly wilts and is reluctant to root. Shoots taken from young mother plants root best. They form roots at different temperatures according to the species, but the optimum air temperature for rooting house plants is 20—25 °C (68—77 °F) and 22—28 °C (72—82 °F) for the compost. Use an open compost and keep it constantly moist. A mixture of peat and perlite or peat and vermiculite makes a suitable rooting compost. Keep up the humidity of the air as unrooted cuttings cannot absorb much water. Insert the cuttings in boxes, or pots 6—9 cm (2$^1/_2$—3$^1/_2$ in) in diameter and put them in a propagating case. Shade them well until they root. The light intensity can be increased later to suit the particular plant's requirements.

Clump-forming plants can be propagated by division. After dividing them, keep the atmosphere moister and warmer for a while. Cover the plants, preferably with plastic sheet.

13

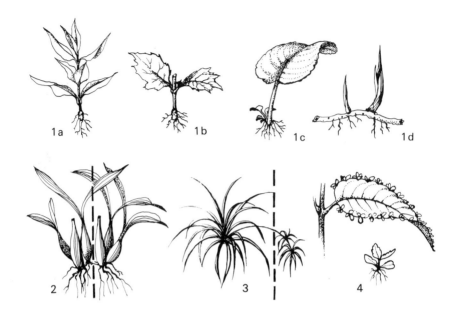

The most widely used ways of propagating indoor plants:
1 — cuttings: a) tip cutting, b) stem cutting, c) leaf cutting,
 d) root cutting
2 — division of clump-forming plant (here orchid pseudo-bulbs)
3 — offshoots
4 — using plantlets formed on some plants' leaves, as *Bryophyllum daigremontianum* here.

Some plants, such as the sword fern and spider plant, produce leaves or shoots with young plants growing at their ends. These young plants can be cut off and planted in small pots.

Some fern species, such as spleenwort (*Asplenium bulbiferum*) form young plants from adventitious buds round the margins of older leaves. These can be collected when large enough and planted in a seed tray to grow on.

As indoor plants are seldom propagated from bulbs, tubers or grafts, these techniques are described, if necessary, under the plant concerned.

GENERAL CARE

Watering

Correct watering is one of the most important aspects of house plant care. It seldom needs to be done daily, but the amount of water given depends on various factors, particularly the air temperature. The higher the temperature, the higher the rate of evaporation of water from the plants and therefore the higher their demands for water. This is commonly true in well lit rooms where the humidity is low. But during autumn and winter when there is less light, watering should be done more cautiously, even if the temperature is reasonable. If the temperature falls below the optimum range, water plants sparingly, whatever the time of year.

The amount of water given to a plant depends on the species and its age. Mature plants should be given large amounts of water at longer intervals, while young plants require frequent watering in smaller doses. Some plants demand constantly moist compost, but others thrive on occasional moistening of the root ball.

If plants are partially dormant, whatever the time of year, water them sparingly. Species which have alternate active and dormant periods, should not be watered at all while dormant. Plants grown in porous clay pots should be watered more frequently than those in glazed pottery or plastic containers. Use water at about room temperature.

Misting and Syringing

We mist or syringe our plants' foliage to reduce the evaporation of water and to make the microclimate more humid. Dry air is one of the most frequent causes of suffering or dying house plants. Use clear water that is not too cold for misting and do the job early enough in the day to ensure that the foliage does not stay wet at night to help avoid trouble from fungal diseases. Keep the flowers dry when misting. Various kinds of sprayer with fine jets are used for both misting and syringing.

Shading

We cannot, of course, use the same shading methods indoors as in a greenhouse. So shade-loving plants are provided with suitable conditions by standing them where they are exposed to the east to north-east or west to north-west. Species that demand more shade should be stood further from the window. Large glassed-in areas and flower windows can be shaded with venetian blinds.

Repotting

Unless planted in a large area of soil in a winter garden or greenhouse, house plants have only limited space in their pots to form a root ball. The compost is therefore less able to hold enough nutrients, water and air and is more likely to lose its good physical properties. Repotting is therefore an indispensable part of the long-term cultivation of plants indoors.

Some fast-growing plants need repotting every year, young ones even twice a year. Other slow-growing or bulky plants are repotted once in two, three or more years. The intervals indicated for repotting the plants described in this book are based on practical experience acquired by growing plants in average indoor conditions, but each plant should be considered individually, as each has its own time for repotting. Examine its state of health, the amount of new growth and the extent to which it has become pot-bound.

But don't wait until you see the first signs of damage to its roots or aerial growth following the deterioration of the physical, chemical and biological properties of the compost. Be sure to repot a plant by the time it has developed a dense network of fine rootlets and formed a compact ball of roots.

The pot or other container chosen for repotting should be only slightly larger than the one it replaces. Small or medium-sized plants should be moved into pots 1—3 cm ($^1/_2$—1 in) larger than before.

The right way to repot a house plant.

Larger plants, repotted after a longer interval, can have a pot 4—8 cm (1½—3 in) bigger. Using too large a pot is wrong as the plant cannot root through the whole layer of soil, which then becomes waterlogged.

Do not remove the old soil from the roots. Only take away the surface layer of soil around the neck of the plant which contains no roots. Put a 2—3 cm (¾—1 in) deep layer of drainage material, such as shingle, gravel, fired clay granules or pot crocks in the bottom of the new container, leaving the drainage hole open. Follow with a thin layer of compost, then stand the root ball in the centre. Fill with soil and press down lightly with your fingers or a wooden rammer. The crown of the plant should be at the same height as before. Leave a 1—3 cm (½—1 in) space, according to the size of the plant, between the surface of the compost and the rim of the pot to allow for watering.

The best time of year for repotting is spring, but some plants can be moved into larger pots in late summer as well. It is best to pot as the next burst of growth is about to begin. Increase the temperature and humidity after repotting but water cautiously. It pays to give smaller amounts at shorter intervals.

Feeding and Fertilisers

Our house plants' feeding requirements vary according to the phase of development. The period of intense growth puts the greatest demand on feeding. Requirements should be met by reasonable doses of ready-made fertilisers, as the soil contains only a minimum of nutrients and plants quickly use them up. If, for example, a plant is repotted into a good compost that contains no fertiliser, there will be only a temporary improvement in its growth and development. After 3—5 weeks the first signs of starvation will be visible. So when preparing soil mixtures it is essential to add granular or powdered fertilisers.

One can buy small packs of fertilisers specially for making up potting composts. Use as directed by the manufacturer. Additional feeding, during the growing season, can be by means of proprietary liquid house plant fertilisers, again used as directed by the maker.

Pruning

Some kinds of house plant need pinching or pruning at a particular phase of growth. Pruning an Indian azalea, rose heath, spotted laurel or poinsettia encourages it to branch and form a more compact plant. Correct pinching results in top quality flowers on chrysanthemums. Soft growth can be cut with a knife, but woody shoots on shrubby plants should be trimmed with sharp secateurs.

Arrangement and Display of Decorative Plants Indoors

When arranging plants indoors particular attention should be paid to the conditions of the room. Choose plants carefully to suit the specific light, temperature and humidity conditions.

Flower windows provide particularly favourable conditions for the growth and development of plants.

The size of the room and its function play an important part in the choice. Single trailing plants are often grown in small rooms, and placed straight on the furniture, windowsills or shelves. Aromatic plants are not suitable for studies and bedrooms. Avoid all flowering,

Epiphytic bromeliads, orchids, cacti, etc. can be grown, as in nature, on tree branches. This is quite an impressive way of displaying house plants, but tending them is rather demanding. Cover the roots of the plants with sphagnum moss and attach the root balls to the branch with thin copper wire or nylon line.

spiny or poisonous plants in children's rooms. Many plants only occasionally thrive in the kitchen.

The most favourable conditions for growing house plants are found in living rooms and entrance halls where there is direct light. Here plants can be arranged in groups of different sizes, though good-sized specimen plants can also be enjoyed. Try grouping several different species in a single ceramic pot. Grouping makes them easier to look after, provided the plants you put together have similar requirements, particularly as regards watering.

A flower window or window greenhouse is a special feature arranged directly in the window frame. A flower window should be at least 50 cm (20 in) wide. This space can be locally heated, probably by heating cables arranged under the cultivating table. It should be possible to ventilate and shade it as necessary too. The interior part of the flower window can be left open, but plants prefer fully glassed-in spaces.

Glass plant-cases (terrariums) are closed glass boxes in which you can create the best conditions for cultivating house plants. Ventilation, supplementary lighting and heating can be provided. As humidity can be kept high, even the demanding species can be grown here.

A winter garden is a spacious glassed-in area, usually forming part of the living room of a family house, a big hall or club room. Always consult an interior designer, interior decorator and garden planner when planning one of these ambitious features.

Pests, Diseases and Protection

To limit troubles from diseases and pests, the indoor gardener should create the best possible growing conditons for his or her plants to suit their specific needs. This is the only way to achieve steady development and healthy growth and with these increased resistance to any kind of disease.

In average indoor conditions plants are exposed to harmful influences from the local microclimate, the macroclimate outdoors, and from the soil. These negative factors, perhaps aggravated by the indoor gardener's inadequate knowledge, can result in poorly timed plant care. The plants then suffer from disorders and their resistance to various pests and diseases is lowered.

Plant troubles have two main groups of causes:
1. Non-living or environmental factors, such as unfavourable light or temperature, a lack or excess of water and air humidity, an unsuitable supply of nutrients for the plant's level of growth, harmful chemicals in the air or water, or a compost whose physical, chemical or biological properties do not suit the plant.
2. Living factors, including pathological fungi, bacteria and pests.

Non-living Causes of Disease

If plants are placed too far from the source of light, the light deficiency shows itself by abnormally long weak growth and foliage that gradually turns yellow, is stunted and falls. This condition can be aggravated by excessive or fluctuating temperatures during the winter.

Excessive light damages shade-loving plants in particular. The amount of new growth is reduced and their leaves gradually fade. Direct sunlight produces yellow mottling on the leaves, which gradually turn brown, dry out and later fall. Even light-loving plants exposed to direct sunlight without first being gradually acclimatised to it, react with reddening leaves (azalea, cacti) and even sun scorch (sansevieria, asparagus) can occur.

Insufficient warmth hinders plants' growth and development and increases their susceptibility to fungus diseases. Their leaves usually turn yellow and at very low temperatures, dark mushy spots appear in plants whose tissues contain a lot of water.

Excessive temperatures are usually accompanied by a decrease in air humidity. Plants then release more water than they can possibly receive through their roots, and their leaves curl, turn yellow and fall.

With underwatering, the aerial parts of the plant wilt and dry out and leaves, buds and flowers drop off. Another symptom of shortage of water in the soil is drying out of the tips of the leaves. An excess of water displaces the air in the soil pores and hinders the roots' respiration. In permanently waterlogged compost, roots rot at low temperatures and die off. The base of the plant can be attacked by a bacterial disease as in sansevieria and dieffenbachia, leaves turn yellow and fall.

Low air humidity (dry air) particularly damages plants from tropical rainforests. Their foliage wilts and drops off. Dry air in centrally-heated homes encourages the multiplication of red spiders and tarsonemid mites.

A decrease or fluctuation in temperature together with high air humidity can bring about yellow mottling and corkiness in leaves of plants grown in closed spaces, such as glass plant cases and winter gardens. High air humidity promotes the spread of various fungus diseases and eelworms (nematodes) attacking the leaves.

A shortage of nutrients in the soil solution inhibits the growth and development of all parts of the plant. Extension growth and foliage are stunted. Later, dark spots appear, though the veins remain a dark green. The plants flower poorly and bear no fruit. If essential nutrients are missing permanently plants will decline and die.

Overfeeding, especially with nitrogen, brings about lush growth of plant tissues and lowered resistance to fungus diseases and pest attacks. Unless the level of nitrogen is balanced with a sufficient amount of phosphorus and potash plants will not flower and make only feeble growth.

Watering with water that contains harmful chemicals such as chlorine, can damage sensitive orchids, azaleas or heaths. Plants do not tolerate the presence of town gas, sulphur dioxide and carbon monoxide. Excessive amounts of these substances cause leaf curl and leaf fall, sometimes even the sudden death of plants. High concentrations of pesticides can also damage parts of plants beyond recovery.

Unsuitable compost inhibits the growth and development of roots and consequently the proper nourishment of plants and their water supply. Besides the physical properties of the soil — the size of soil particles, water capacity and air content, permeability and heating capacity — its chemical reaction expressed in pH is of great importance.

Living Organisms that Cause Disease

Fungal diseases attack almost all plant species and organs. The infection is spread by soil, water, affected parts of plants, spores and sometimes even on seeds. Fungus diseases are seen in germinating and young plants that become weak and fall over, in wilting leaves, rotting roots, necks and aerial organs, as well as mottling and coating in different colours, particularly brown or grey. Plants grown in low or fluctuating temperatures and humid atmospheres are the most frequently attacked. Fungus diseases can be prevented by disinfecting the soil and affected plants, ventilating generously with some supplementary heating, especially during the damp autumn months, and adequate watering and feeding of plants. Treat infected plants with fungicides based on benomyl or thiophanate-methyl.

Virus diseases affect the leaves, flowers and stems as well as the bulbs or tubers of ornamental plants. Viruses show themselves in different ways. The most frequent symptoms are leaf and stem mosaics with characteristic light or dark green spots arranged in circles or stripes. Sometimes the leaf blades are curled or frilled. Attacked tissues gradually die and the plant is stunted. Flowers are in different colours and do not develop normally, so they are neither decorative nor do they reproduce.

Viruses are easily carried to healthy plants by sucking insects such as aphids, thrips and whitefly, or mechanically perhaps on a knife, when tending plants.

Strict preventive measures should be observed to protect plants from virus diseases. Only propagate from healthy mother plants. Be sure to disinfect tools like scissors and knives in alcohol or formalin. Do not forget to wash your hands too. The sucking insects should be destroyed and infested parts removed and burnt immediately the disease is discovered. Also make sure your plants are properly fed.

Bacteria can attack parts of plants and are very difficult to cure. They generally attack parts that have been mechanically damaged or appear on plants weakened by unfavourable growing conditions. In so-called systemic diseases, bacteria spread through the vascular bundles and affect the whole plant so it wilts, turns brown and dies. Such diseases are practically incurable.

Bacteria can cause damp or dry rot by decaying the soft tissues on stems, leaves, flowers, bulbs and tubers. The lower parts of stems and roots can be attacked by bacteria which cause an unnatural proliferation of cells that form tumours or galls on the parts attacked.

The best way to protect our plants from bacterial infection is to tend them conscientiously and create the best conditions for their growth. Weak, sick and damaged plants should be removed promptly since treating bacterial diseases is most unsuccessful.

Insect pests infest all plant species when conditions favour their distribution. Aphids damage leaves, stems and flowers by sucking the sap from the cells. Damaged parts become twisted and distorted. Aphids multiply in a dry and warm environment. Preventive measures include adequate humidity, spraying and misting the plants with water, as well as good ventilation. Use chemical preparations based on dimethoate, pirimicarb or malathion.

Red spider mites appear first on the undersurface of leaves, causing fine, whitish to yellow mottling by sucking their sap. In a dry, warm microclimate they spread rapidly to all aerial parts of the plant, considerably weakening it. Leaves and flowers are coated with fine cobwebs. Increasing atmospheric humidity and lowering the temperature reduces the reproduction of red spider mites. They can be eradicated with dimethoate, malathion, derris or pirimiphos-methyl.

Thrips damage plants by sucking the cell sap and infecting them with poisonous substances. Damaged parts become frilled and dry out. If the attack is severe, plants can die. A dry, warm environment encourages the proliferation of thrips. Preventive measures are similar to those for red spider mites. Use chemicals such as malathion, dimethoate or derris.

Whitefly, both mature insects and larvae, suck the juices mainly from the underside of the leaves. Plants become polluted with their excrement and secreted honeydew. Whitefly occur at higher temperatures in both dry and humid atmospheres. Spray with preventive chemicals 3 or 4 times at weekly intervals, to get rid of the eggs and larvae, which can be rather resistant to treatment, as well as the mature insects. Use permethrin or dimethoate.

Cyst nematodes or eelworms (Heterodera) attack roots, bulbs, tubers, stems and leaves of ornamental plants. They produce galls of irregular or globular shape. Watery blotches, which later turn brown or black, appear on the leaves and stems. Various parts of the plant are deformed or die. Heterodera are carried by the soil, water and tools, so infected plants should not be sprayed, and feeding with nitrogen should be limited.

Tarsonemid mites damage buds, leaves and stems of plants by sucking. Infested parts are gradually deformed or stunted and later turn brown, corky and die off. The pests reproduce well in humid conditions, so the humidity should be reduced by ventilation. Spray with insecticides several times.

Scale insects suck the sap from the leaves and stem cells and parts of the plant then fade or are distorted. Armoured scales and mealy bugs are most frequently encountered on ornamental plants. They attack palms, cacti and woody species in particular. Besides treating scale insects with chemicals they should also be removed by hand. Repeated spraying and washing the plants with malathion or dimethoate is the most effective control.

It is vitally important to follow the instructions given on the container when using chemical preparations.

Other pests that attack ornamental plants include springtails, slugs and snails and earwigs. It pays to consult an expert if you are in any doubt when trying to identify a disease or pest, as it is often difficult to identify the true cause of the trouble.

COLOUR PLATES

Chenille Plant, Red-hot Cat's Tail

Acalypha hispida

Euphorbiaceae

A variety of species of Acalypha remain native to the tropical regions of all parts of the world. They are mostly shrubs or herbs with conspicuously variegated leaves. *Acalypha hispida* (1) has oval, pointed, dark green leaves and decorative drooping inflorescences, red or white in colour and often 30−50 cm (12−20 in) long. By crossing *A. hispida* with *A. godseffiana* we now have cultivars with pink, greenish white, yellowish green and bronze flowers.

These plants need a minimum temperature of 18−20 °C (64−68 °F) in winter and sufficient light. In summer, they should be protected from strong sunshine. They can be grown in an equal parts mixture of leaf-mould, soil-based potting compost and peat at pH 5.5−6.5. Repotting should be done between March and July when temperatures rise above 20 °C (68 °F), but watering should be restricted during winter. Syringe the leaves in summer. From February to August, feed the plant with a compound fertiliser solution at ten day intervals.

Chenille plants are propagated from tip cuttings (2) between March and July. Insert three to five cuttings in 8−10 cm (3−4 in) diameter pots containing an equal parts mixture of peat and leaf-mould. Stand them in a warm, slightly shaded spot with high air humidity, preferably under polythene sheeting and gently mist them every day. When the plants have rooted, gradually harden them off and move them to a permanent spot.

3

The Chenille Plant is a temporary decorative indoor plant. Of the variegated species and cultivars, the Beefsteak Plant, *Acalypha wilkesiana* 'Musaica' (3), is occasionally grown. It has bronze green leaves with crimson stripes. Other species and cultivars with more conspicuously coloured leaves are encountered in some botanical garden collections, but they are not important for indoor cultivation.

Mature plants are grown in large pots or ceramic bowls in a warm and rather humid atmosphere. They can be planted in flower windows and winter gardens. The lower leaves fall from older plants if the atmosphere is not humid enough.

1

2

27

Hot Water Plant
Achimenes hybrids

Gesneriaceae

These fragile, rather fleshy herbs originate in the tropics of Mexico and Central and South America. The plant is not commonly grown in European homes, because of its long alternating periods of vegetative growth and complete dormancy. This makes considerable demands on the gardener's time and skills. Achimenes flowers from June to August, with blue, pink or white blooms or combinations of these colours in some hybrids. Most of the hybrids have been derived from the pure botanical species, *A. longiflora* and *A. grandiflora.* Small, rather popular hybrids belong to the 'Little Beauty' group, as for instance 'Cockade' (1), 'Mexicana' (2), and 'Fancy' (3).

Achimenes is grown in warm or fairly warm rooms at temperatures from 16 to 24 °C (61—75 °F) and slightly shaded. It needs a coarse textured compost produced by mixing 1 part young leafmould with 1 part fibrous peat and ⅓ part perlite with a pH of 5.5—6.5. During the non-flowering period plants should be well-watered and their leaves should be misted carefully. Constant, moist compost is a must during the flowering period. The plants are fed from March to July.

Achimenes is propagated from its tubers or tip cuttings in February and March. Several small tubers are planted 1 cm (½ in) deep in a 10—12 cm (4—5 in) diameter pot. Only three-quarters fill the pot with soil, then top it up after the stem emerges.

Reducing watering during autumn forces the plants to stop growing. Their tubers should be stored in dry peat or sand in a room at about 15 °C (59 °F) in winter.

The large flowered hybrids make lush growth and can be either tied up or grown as drooping basket plants. They can be grown on verandas, in windows, other than those facing south, on epiphytic trunks and branches in winter gardens and in glass plant-cases. Though each blossom only lasts for a short time, the plants flower profusely and are highly ornamental.

3

2

1

Urn Plant
Aechmea fasciata

Bromeliaceae

Aechmea fasciata (1), which grows as an epiphyte is native to Brazil. Its wide leaves with striking silvery stripes are arranged in a rosette or vase, which forms a water-cistern. A long-lasting inflorescence with pink bracts grows from the centre of the rosette. Its roots are not strongly developed so pots about 10 cm (4 in) in diameter are large enough for it. This plant thrives in centrally-heated homes.

The Urn Plant should be slightly shaded and grown at a temperature from 18 to 25 °C (64—77 °F) in summer. The plants should be given as much light as possible in winter. They will not be harmed by a short exposure to direct sunlight either. Plant them in well-drained, airy compost of a rather coarse texture, such as a blend of 2 parts fibrous peat, to 1 part of chipped bark and 1 of perlite with a pH value of 5.0—5.5. Do not repot plants with faded flowers. Use any sideshoots for propagation in July and August. They root if slightly shaded in an equal parts mixture of peat and sand at temperatures over 22 °C (72 °F) with maximum air humidity.

The Urn Plant should be watered with soft water. In summer, pour the water into the leaf rosette as well as in the pot, but when temperatures are lower, only moisten the compost. Spray over the leaves at flowering time. Supplementary feeding should be done cautiously, using a quarter strength solution of house plant fertiliser from February to October.

2

Apart from *A. fasciata,* one also comes across the lovely *A. chantinii* (2). This species has striking silvery grey stripes on its leaves and a red-bracted inflorescence. *A. fulgens* (3), which is less often seen has violet-purple flowers on a long-lasting inflorescence.

Brown mottling of the leaves or drying of the leaf tips is sometimes seen in urn plants. Unsuitable temperature is usually the cause of this trouble.

Urn plants are very versatile. They can be displayed as specimen plants or grouped into ceramic bowls. They often

1

3

serve as basic material for epiphytic
trunks and branches. Flower-windows
glassed-in on one side, and winter
gardens are ideal places to grow urn
plants.

Aeschynanthus, Zebra Basket Vine
Aeschynanthus marmoratus

Gesneriaceae

The various species of Aeschynanthus originated from the islands of Indonesia. But of almost 200 species described, only six or eight are used in ornamental horticulture. The Zebra Basket Vine (1) is a trailing species with opposite light green leaves decorated on underside with conspicuous brown-violet stripes. The flowers are an interesting shape but an inconspicuous green-brown colour and have only a short life.

The plants thrive in winter temperatures of 18−22 °C (64−72 °F) and slight shade. They can tolerate short-term falls in temperature. Only repot well-rooted plants between February and June. Do not remove the old soil when repotting and cover the plants with light plastic sheet for 10−14 days. Use a compost of 1 part coarse peat, 1 part half-decomposed leafmould (or pine bark) and ½ part sand with a pH of 5−5.5.

The plants should be well watered frequently during the summer, and profusely syringed. During the winter limit watering or leaf fall could result. Feed the plants from March to October.

Propagation is quite easy. Insert five to seven mature stem cuttings with two or three pairs of leaves each in a 10 cm (4 in) pot (2). They root in compost at a temperature of 24−26 °C (75−79 °F) and high air humidity (3).

3

The Zebra Basket Vine is mainly used for decorating closed flower windows, plant-cases and epiphytic trunks in winter gardens.

A. speciosus has orange flowers and leaves that are green on both sides.

A. radicans with bright red flowers and

2

32

red-brown calyx used to be more widely grown than it is now.

All kinds of *Aeschynanthus* need daily attention and care. They are not happy in centrally-heated homes.

1

Ribbon Aglaonema

Araceae

Aglaonema commutatum 'Pseudobracteatum'

Aglaonemas, or Chinese evergreens, come from the Indonesian rain-forests. They are fairly slow to grow whether in a greenhouse or centrally-heated homes. One of the most widespread cultivars is *Aglaonema commutatum* 'Pseudobracteatum' (1), reminiscent of dieffenbachia by its leaf shape as well as height. It grows 50−60 cm (20−24 in) high. Its short main stem carries narrow, lanceolate dark green leaves with a creamy variegation.

Two-year-old plants can produce their first inconspicuous inflorescences, usually during the winter. The spathe is greenish white and the spadix almost white. If it develops fruits these are orange-red and ornamental (2) and decorate the plant for 3−4 months.

Aglaonemas are grown at 18−24 °C (64−75 °F) during the winter. They do not demand light conditions so can be grown quite a way from a window. Pot them in the same soil mixture as dieffenbachias. Repot the plants, if necessary, between March and September. The soil should be kept moist, but not waterlogged. The plants thrive in rather high air humidity. Feed them from the end of February until October.

The plants are best propagated by division in early spring, which is best carried out when repotting. The Aglaonema seed ripens even in indoor conditions and should be sown immediately it is harvested.

Aglaonema commutatum 'Treubii' (3) has a similar habit to the ribbon aglaonema, but has dark green leaves with a grey pattern. A less important species, *Aglaonema costatum,* has a short stem and oval, emerald-green leaves with a striking white-yellow midrib and white variegation. The Painted Drop Tongue, *A. crispum,* has stiffer, oval dark green leaves with a silvery-grey pattern. It grows very slowly.

Aglaonemas are long-lived plants that can be grown as specimens or grouped in ceramic bowls with other plants that have similar needs. They tolerate quite shady spots so they can be grown successfully where most house plants fail because of the poor light.

1

Voodoo Plant, Devil's Tongue
Amorphophallus rivieri

Araceae

Amorphophallus originates from tropical East Asia and the Indonesian islands. In indoor conditions, the plant generally reaches a height of 80−100 cm (31−39 in). The stem of a single light green leaf with a feathery (pinnate) blade (2) springs up from the tuber (1). The leaf only begins to sprout when the inflorescence with its dark violet spathe and spadix has shed its blossoms (3).

The tubers should be stored dry at 15−17 °C (59−63 °F). In February or March they can be pre-sprouted in pure peat at 22−24 °C (72−75 °F) or potted straight in an 11−14 cm (4−5½ in) pot, depending on the size of the tuber. Fill the pot with an equal parts mixture of peat and soil-based potting compost with a pH value of 5.5−6.5. The potting compost should be well drained and aerated. When the tubers have sprouted, lower the temperature to 20−22 °C (68−72 °F) and water the slightly shaded plants generously.

Amorphophallus needs feeding from March to August, once every 7−10 days. Cease watering in October and when the plant has stopped growing lift the tubers, clean them and store them carefully until spring.

In summer, *Amorphophallus rivieri* can be grown on balconies, open verandas or even in garden beds. But direct sunshine can scorch the leaves, so it is best to keep the plants slightly shaded.

4

Amorphophallus titanum (4) used to be grown in limited quantities in nurseries. But it is up to 5 metres (16 ft) tall, so is only suitable for large greenhouses.

This fast-growing plant does quite well in flats, offices and corridors. Its tubers are poisonous. It is unlikely to be more widely grown because of the strong foetid smell of its flower. Never grow amorphophallus in bedrooms or rooms with poor ventilation and make sure it is not touched by children.

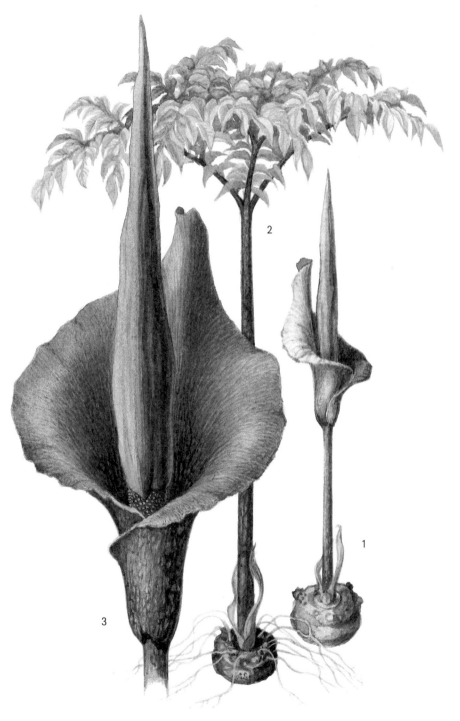

Pineapple
Ananas comosus 'Variegatus'

Bromeliaceae

The pineapple is native to Brazil, but has spread as an edible plant to the tropics in all parts of the world. But it is rarely found growing indoors as an ornamental plant.

Ananas comosus 'Variegatus' (1) has stiff, spiny leaves arranged in a rosette. The leaf coloration is rather variable. The white-striped leaf margins sometimes have a pinkish tinge. Given good light a pink to red colouring is more widespread over the leaf. The flowers are small and inconspicuous, but the compound fruit (2), is quite showy and will ripen even in a greenhouse, flower window or glass plant-case.

The pineapple grows happily in a winter temperature of 20—22 °C (68—72 °F) but it demands good light so it should be grown close to the window, except for young plants being rooted, which need slight shade. The pineapple thrives in a mixture of 1 part half-decomposed leafmould, 1 part peat and 1/2 part sand at pH 5.0—5.5.

Water regularly, using water which is left to stand overnight. The plant can be misted over from time to time. It needs feeding occasionally from March to October with a 1/4 strength solution of liquid house plant fertiliser.

Propagate the pineapple from its sideshoots which root in a mixture of peat and sand at high air humidity and a soil temperature of 26—30 °C (79—86 °F). Selected offshoots should be strong enough to root in an 8—10 cm (3—4 in) pot. Pineapples can also be propagated by cutting off the leaf rosette at the top of a ripe compound fruit (3).

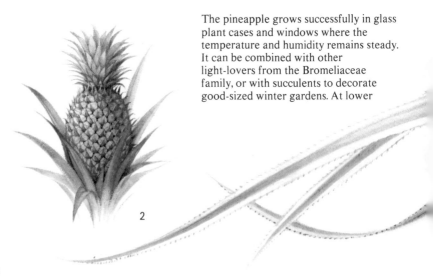

The pineapple grows successfully in glass plant cases and windows where the temperature and humidity remains steady. It can be combined with other light-lovers from the Bromeliaceae family, or with succulents to decorate good-sized winter gardens. At lower

2

temperatures in winter, cut down
watering, but in summer lack of water
can dry out the leaf tips.
   Pineapples have also been grown
successfully in hydroponic solutions. In
poor light the plant will not flower and its
leaves will not colour well.

1

3

Flame Plant, Flamingo Flower
Anthurium scherzerianum — hybrids

Araceae

Anthuriums are native to Central and South America. Some species of this genus are grown only for their decorative foliage because they have inconspicuous flowers. *A. scherzerianum* and *A. andreanum* gave rise to several valuable varieties. Their many hybrids are distinguished by lovely colourful flowers; the two species, however, cannot be crossed.

Anthurium scherzerianum hybrids (1) form clumps with dark green leathery lanceolate leaves. The flower stalk can be up to 30 cm (12 in) high and bears a spirally twisted spadix and an oval spathe, which can be orange, red, pink or almost white.

Anthuriums are grown in slight shade, at winter temperatures of 18 to 22 °C (64 — 72 °F). The compost should have a coarse open texture to let through air and water. It can be prepared by mixing fibrous peat together with pine bark, perlite, and moss peat. The pH value should be 4.5 — 5. The plants are best repotted between February and August.

Water the plants with soft water left to stand overnight, the amount depending on the air temperature and the condition of the compost. In summer, mist over the plants frequently. Feed them from February to October.

In greenhouses, anthuriums are propagated from seeds sown in peat. Indoors, the plant can be divided and the divisions planted separately in the basic potting compost.

2

A. andreanum hybrids (2) were cultivated from the original species, *A. andreanum,* in English called Painter's Palette, or Tail Flower. The hybrids are rather robust, with long, elongated heart-shaped leaves. The flower's spadix is yellowish white and untwisted, the broad cordate spathe usually being red. They are grown almost exclusively as cut flowers.

A. crystallinum has handsome wide ovate, matt leaves with striking silvery-white veins (3). The inflorescence is inconspicuous.

Anthurium is not at all happy in permanetly dry air, but it is good for decorating flower windows, glass plant-cases, winter gardens and shaded greenhouses.

3

1

Zebra Plant
Acanthaceae
Aphelandra squarrosa 'Dania'

Of the several dozen members of the Aphelandra genus that grow in the tropical forests of Central and South America the cultivars of *Aphelandra squarrosa* are almost the only ones grown as ornamentals. *A. squarrosa* 'Dania' (1) ranks among the most valuable, its dark green leaves having striking, silvery-green veins (2). The bracts of its flower spike are yellow. This plant grows about 30−50 cm (12−20 in) high indoors.

Aphelandra should be grown in partial shade, as it can be damaged by direct sunlight. On the other hand poor light in winter inhibits more intense growth and flower formation. The winter temperature should not be allowed to fall below 18 °C (64 °F) for long. The optimum temperature ranges from 20 to 24 °C (68−75 °F) with high humidity.

Pot this plant in a light, airy soil-based compost, such as 1 part leafmould mixed with 1 part peat, 1 part soil-based potting compost and ½ part sand with a pH of 5−6. The plant should be repotted into a 2 cm (¾ in) larger pot between March and May.

Liberal watering is desirable during the summer, but should be withheld at lower temperatures. An excess or a lack of water can both cause leaf-fall. Syringe plants whenever possible during the summer. Feed aphelandras from March to August. After the plant has finished flowering, cut off the rest of the inflorescence and lower the temperature and reduce watering from October right through to February.

This plant is propagated from tip cuttings inserted into small (7 cm/2½ in) pots filled with a peat and sand mixture. They root best in high humidity with a soil temperature of about 25 °C (77 °F).

Aphelandras can be infested by aphids, tarsonemid mites and scale insects. Soil fungi can damage the root and wilt the foliage.

It can be risky to stand the plants outside closed cases and windows as they are not too tolerant of poor growing conditions. They often do better in a hydroponic solution than in an orthodox soil compost.

2

1

Norfolk Island Pine
Araucaria heterophylla

Araucariaceae

Norfolk Island, off the east coast of Australia, is the home of the 'indoor fir', *Araucaria heterophylla* (1). This woody plant with branches arranged in whorls is not often grown in modern homes, as it is rather demanding in the kind of environment it will thrive in.

Araucaria should pass the winter at low temperatures from 6 to 10 °C (43−45 °F) in a well-lit room with a humid atmosphere. Dry air and high winter temperatures result in yellowing and drying out of its needle-like leaves. Araucaria will tolerate full sunlight only occasionally, in well-ventilated rooms or grown outside during the summer, after it has been hardened off.

Grow it in an open soil-based compost such as John Innes potting compost No. 2. Araucarias can be repotted between March and June. Do not remove the old soil from the root ball, and pot the plant at the same depth as was in its previous pot.

Watering should be ample and regular but limited from October to February. Once a week is sufficient during this period. It will become dormant at low temperatures. Feed the plant from April to August with a liquid fertiliser solution.

2

Propagating araucarias indoors from imported seeds (2) is rather difficult. It is better to rely on specialised nurseries.

Araucarias are suitable for decorating spacious rooms with low or fluctuating winter temperatures and high humidity, such as light entrance halls and corridors where large specimen plants can be stood.

Cultivating this tree in a hydroponic solution produces problems, so only very experienced gardeners are likely to succeed.

1

Asparagus Fern
Asparagus densiflorus 'Sprengeri'

Liliaceae

Asparagus densiflorus 'Sprengeri' (1) is widely distributed all round the Mediterranean and has been cultivated as a domestic plant for a very long time. The drooping shoots of older plants reach more than 1 m (3ft 3in) in length. Plants as young as two years can flower, producing tiny white blossoms (2).

Asparagus can be grown in winter temperatures ranging from 5 to 18 °C (41 − 64 ° F), the optimum being about 12 − 15 °C (54 − 60 ° F). This plant will tolerate fluctuating temperatures but is rather demanding for light, and can be damaged by direct sunlight unless it has been hardened off beforehand.

As asparagus grows very quickly, it needs repotting every year between February and November. Use a rather heavy potting compost, as for example, a mix of 2 parts John Innes potting compost to 1 of peat, or equal parts of loam and peat. The pH value should be adjusted to 6.0 − 7.0. Plants need more frequent watering in summer but in winter are content with a low water-supply. The dry air in centrally-heated homes can cause the leaflets to yellow and drop off.

Asparagus demands a lot of nourishment, so feed fortnightly in summer with a house plant fertiliser.

Asparagus is easily propagated by division or by seeds sown in an equal parts mix of peat and sand in early spring.

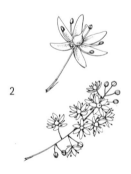

2

The Asparagus Fern, *A. setaceus* (3), has soft, bristle-like leaflets. It requires a more humid atmosphere and half shade, and is grown at temperatures above 15 °C (60 °F). *A. densiflorus* 'Myers' (4) grows more slowly, its shoots reaching about 50 cm (20 in) in length.

Asparagus Ferns can be used to decorate places heated to a temperature of about 12 − 18 °C (54 − 64 °F), such as corridors, staircases and halls. Glassed-in entrance rooms with fluctuating temperatures due to frequent ventilation, are suitable for an arrangement of asparagus as well. In summer, they can be planted among flowering plants like geraniums in window boxes and bowls, used to decorate windows and balconies.

1

4

3

47

Aspidistra
Aspidistra elatior

Liliaceae

The aspidistra was brought to Europe from Japan in the first half of the last century and spread rapidly, because it was so undemanding and adaptable. *A. elatior* has dark green leathery oblong lanceolate leaves with long petioles. The plant flowers irregularly, producing inconspicuous, dull purple flowers at soil level (2).

Aspidistra will stand very low winter temperatures, from 4 to 12 °C (39 — 54 °F). In summer it can be easily grown on balconies or in the open garden, provided it is never in direct sunlight. Prepare a suitable compost by mixing 2 parts of soil-based compost with 1 part peat at pH 6.0 — 7.5. Aspidistras dislike frequent repotting, so do this only once in 2 — 3 years between March and May.

Young plants require frequent watering, but older ones need water only once in two or three days. During the winter watering should be limited according to room temperature. Only syringe while cuttings are rooting. These should be cut away from the roots together with a single leaf. The most favourable periods for rooting are March to April and August to September. Stand the rooting plants in a room where the temperature doesn't fall below 20 °C (68 °F). Use a compound liquid fertiliser solution for supplementary feeding from March to August.

Aspidistra elatior 'Variegata' (1) whose leaves are striped white or creamy-white, needs more heat and a winter temperature from 16 to 18 °C (61 — 64 °F).

Aspidistras can be grown even in the most unfavourable conditions, as they can stand up to deep shade, fluctuating temperatures, dust and draught. So they can be stood in poorly lit corridors and entrance halls.

2

48

1

In a cold and humid environment dark blotches of fungal origin can appear on the foliage. Aspidistras are also sometimes attacked by red spider mite in a dry environment. But such occurrences are rare since aspidistras rank among the hardiest of house plants.

Asplenium, Bird's Nest Fern, Shuttlecock   Polypodiaceae
Asplenium nidus

The tropics of Asia and Australia are home to the Bird's Nest Fern, *Asplenium nidus* (1). It is not very amenable to dry atmospheres as it is short-lived as a house plant. Its fast-growing, glossy, light green leaves with a black midrib are arranged in a funnel-shaped rosette. They grow up to 80 — 100 cm (31 — 39 in) long. Older plants bear many sporangia on the undersides of leaves which produce the spores by which the plants reproduce. During the winter they require temperatures of about 20 — 24 °C (68 — 75 °F) and slight shade. The temperature should never fall below 18 °C (64 °F). In summer, the bird's nest fern should be grown in partial shade where its foliage is protected against the effects of direct sunlight.

The compost used should be airy and porous, yet retain sufficient water to stay moist. A mix of 1 part leafmould, 1 part peat and ¹/₅th part sand of pH 4.5 — 6.5 is most suitable. Repot large plants between March and August. After repotting, keep the air as humid as possible.

Asplenium demands regular watering with soft water at room temperature, that is, above 20 °C (68 °F). Carefully mist over the leaves so that they dry before the evening. Otherwise red-brown mottling could develop.

Once a month, from March to July, give your asplenium a supplementary feed with a compound fertiliser solution. Specialised nurseries propagate these ferns from spores.

2

One often comes across the Mother or New Zealand Spleenwort, *A. bulbiferum* (2) in garden centres. They have finely cut fronds and are more easily propagated by using the young plants that form on their fronds, as well as by spores, than the Bird's Nest Fern. They tolerate quite deep shade.

Asplenium nidus is generally grown in a pot, though in its homeland it grows as epiphyte.

Asplenium ferns have only limited use, as they can only survive about one or two years in average indoor conditions. They do better in well-heated winter gardens or greenhouses where it is easier to keep a sufficiently humid atmosphere.

1

Aucuba, Spotted Laurel
Aucuba japonica 'Variegata'

Cornaceae

Only three species of aucuba grow in the forests of the Himalayas and East Asia. *Aucuba japonica* is the most important in horticulture. The most widely grown cultivar 'Variegata' (1) is a shrub reaching about 1 m (3.3 ft) high in our conditions. It has leathery opposite, dentate and ovate to lanceolate leaves. At present, variegated cultivars with yellow-spotted leaves are grown. Female plants also bear decorative light red, single-seeded berries.

These woody plants are content with a temperature of 15 °C (59 °F) or lower in winter. In summer they grow best in semi-shade, though they can stand deep shade. They are grown in a mixture of 3 parts soil-based compost and 1 part peat at pH 6.0 — 7.5. Young plants need annual repotting between February and May. Older plants need repotting only once in two years.

Aucubas need more frequent watering in summer, but permanently damp compost can cause yellowing foliage. In winter, limit watering to a minimum and do not expose plants to very damp atmospheres or blotches of fungal origin could develop on their leaves. Aucubas should have a supplementary feed every three weeks from April to August, using a solution of compound fertiliser.

Propagation by tip cuttings is best done between February and May or in August. The cuttings root quite easily in peat kept at 22 — 24 °C (72 — 75 °F).

2

Aucubas are planted singly in good-sized containers (2) and used for cool rooms, corridors and foyers. They don't thrive in hot rooms in winter. An excessive air circulation causes leaf fall. These shrubs are easily shaped by pruning and prunings can be used for propagating.

Aucubas are dioecious plants so one must grow male and female plants together to obtain fruits and seeds. In summer, good-sized plants can be stood outside in a partially shaded spot, after they have been gradually hardened off. In autumn, aucubas can stand a fall in temperature to zero. Poorly grown plants can be attacked by aphids and eelworms.

1

Begonia
Begonia Elatior hybrids

Begoniaceae

A large group of *Begonia* Elatior hybrids (1) arose from crossing the natural species *B. socotrana* and the hybrid *Begonia* × *tuberhybrida*. The cultivars grown nowadays are noted for their short compact growth and profuse flowers in pink, orange and red. The flowering time can be regulated.

Plants propagated in spring bear flowers in October and November unless the natural day-length is altered. By regulating their cultivation, they can be flowered in any season of the year.

Begonias are propagated by tip cuttings, which root in the greenhouse at 20 to 25 °C (68 − 77 °F) in about three weeks. Indoors, the flowers can be made to last longer by reducing the temperature to 15 − 18 °C (59 − 64 °F).

Begonias require a uniformly moist compost. Overwatering is harmful when temperatures are low. The foliage can be misted over on warm summer days, but must dry out by the evening. The most suitable compost is a light, permeable medium of equal parts leaf-mould, peat and soil-based compost at pH 6.0.

For supplementary feeding use a compound fertilizer solution. Excessive nitrogen coupled with poor light results in lush growth and soft stem growth.

Begonias will not tolerate direct sunlight, so they should be grown in semi-shade. In summer, some of the more recent cultivars can be grown outside in window boxes or tubs. If temperatures fluctuate widely, begonias will drop their flowers and their leaves.

2

Begonia 'Lorraine' hybrids (2) have very similar cultural requirements. These cultivars have flowers mainly in shades of pink. As begonias only last for a limited time indoors they are only suitable for seasonal decoration.

Begonias with decorative foliage do not do well if the air is dry. Sometimes, *Begonia rex* hybrids (3) as well as *B. masoniana* can be used to decorate flower windows and glassed plant cases where the humidity of the air can be controlled. They do well at 14 to 18 °C (57 − 64 °F) in high humidity. Some of them require a short resting period during the winter.

1

3

Brassaia, Umbrella Tree
Brassaia actinophylla

Araliaceae

The tree-like *B. actinophylla* (1) originally called *Schefflera actinophylla* is widely distributed in the tropics of South-East Asia and Australia. In recent decades some variegated cultivars have also appeared on the market. They have a shrubby habit of growth, reaching a height of 1. 5—2 m (5—6 ft) in indoor conditions. The palmately divided, glossy leathery leaves are a deep green. The species itself is propagated in nurseries from imported seeds. The small-leaved species, such as *S. arboricola* (2) and Seven Fingers, *S. digitata* (3), can be propagated from tip cuttings from March to August. They should be inserted in 7—8 cm (2½—3 in) pots filled with a mixture of leafmould and peat and placed in an air-conditioned propagator. They root at an air temperature of 22—24 °C (72—75 °F) and a compost temperature of 20—22 °C (68—72 °F), preferably covered with a sheet of plastic. Keep a high air humidity.

Brassaias do well in diffused light or partial shade at a temperature of 16—20 °C (61—68 °F). If the air in a room is too dry their bottom leaves will drop off. This is why schleffleras need frequent misting at higher temperatures. During the summer, plants should be watered daily to keep the compost slightly moist, but during the winter the plants should be given more light and the water supply should be reduced.

Repotting is necessary every 1 or 2 years from March to May, preferably in a mixture of 2 parts leafmould, 1 part loam and 1 part peat at a pH of 5.0—6.0 Brassaias should be fed at ten-day intervals from the end of March to August with a solution of compound fertiliser.

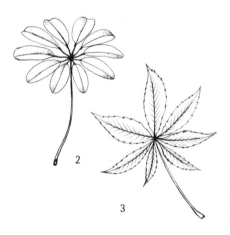

Brassaias have been in great demand as house plants recently. They can be arranged with other plants in large groups and grown in winter gardens or flower windows. They can be grown successfully in individual pots provided the air humidity in the room is at least 60%. Schleffleras also thrive in hydroponics, particularly in good-sized containers like tubs.

1

Brunfelsia
Brunfelsia pauciflora

Brunfelsia (1) forms an erect or arching evergreen shrub with oblong lanceolate, glossy, dark green leaves (2). It is a native of Brazil. The blue, violet to purple flowers arranged in umbels (3) appear from January to April. The wider use of this interesting plant is hampered by the difficulty of propagating it. Tip cuttings root after several months in soil-based compost in a greenhouse at a temperature of about 28−30 °C (82−86 °F), so one is recommended to use hormone rooting powders to encourage rooting. It is practically impossible to propagate brunfelsias indoors.

Plants are grown in temperatures ranging from 15 to 25 °C (59–77°F) in diffused light. Direct sunlight damages the foliage and severe changes of temperature can cause leaf fall. The plants need generous watering and frequent spraying of the foliage while in active growth. Brunfelsias are grown in an acid potting compost with a pH of 4−5.5. Prepare compost by mixing 1 part pine needle mould, 2 parts peat and ½ part loam. Hoof and hornmeal or bonemeal should be added as a fertiliser. While in growth, brunfelsias should receive a supplementary feed every week with a complete fertiliser solution.

The plants are rested in winter by limiting watering and keeping temperatures down to 10−14 °C (50−57 °F), during which time they should be stood in a lighter spot close to a window.

3

Brunfelsias have only limited uses. As they require considerable air humidity, they can be planted singly in plant cases and conservatories. By triming their branches, better branching and more compact growth are produced.

B. pauciflora 'Macrantha' with large flowers is rarely grown. It has similar cultural requirements to the original species.

59

Cacti

Cacti form a dominant part of the vegetation in some North and South American areas. They grow in tropical and sub-tropical steppes and semi-deserts, many of them on mountain rocks, some on trees as epiphytes. Cacti are of columnar, flattened or spherical shape. Their succulent stems are green and often provided with ribs. Almost all cacti lack real leaves. The conspicuously coloured flowers are largely regular or symmetrical in shape. Spines arise from aeroles (4) arranged regularly on the rib ridges or on tubercles.

The prolific Cactaceae family comprises about 200 genera and some 2,000 species of plants. The growing conditions and cultivation required by cacti vary according to the species, so any general rules are only approximate.

Schlumbergera truncata (1), known as the Lobster or Crab Cactus, is indigenous to Brazil. It is propagated by cuttings in August or between January and March. It roots in peat at a temperature of about 22 °C (72 °F). Adult plants are grown in slight shade at 18 to 22 °C (64–72 °F). Lobster Cacti bud best during 8–9 hour days with a night temperature of 15 °C (59 °F). The plant needs small amounts of water as well as an occasional mist from March to August. Encourage formation of buds by limiting watering from mid-August to mid-September. Regular watering should then be continued until the end of the flowering period. After the flowers have been shed, the temperature should be decreased to 15 °C (59 °F). Minimum watering is sufficient till March. The plants should then be repotted in a porous mixture such as equal parts peat and loam with a pH of 5.5–6.5. While in growth schlumbergera should be fed with a compound fertiliser, with high nitrogen at the beginning and later with extra phosphate.

The cultivar 'Winter Tales' (2) bears lighter pink blossoms than the original species.

2

3

4

1

Rhipsalidopsis gaertneri (3) which
flowers in early spring has similar needs.
Its cultivars bear red, pink or orange
flowers, often of different colours inside
and out. In winter, rhipsalidopsis should
be kept in temperatures of 10 – 12 °C
(50 – 54 °F) for about two months. If also
in full light, flower initiation will take
place. After this cool period, the
temperature should be raised to only
16 – 18 °C (61 – 64 °F), as higher
temperatures can cause bud drop.

Cacti should be over-wintered at temperatures from 6 to 10 °C (43−50 °F) in a light place. Most species need full sun in summer, though some should be adapted to it gradually. Cacti should not be watered during the winter months. As the outside temperature increases in spring, the gardener should start careful watering, gradually increasing the dosage. When moistening the compost, make sure that the aerial part of the plant is kept dry.

Prepare a suitable compost for cacti by mixing grit or coarse sand with John Innes potting compost. Remember to put in a generous layer of drainage material first, such as crushed brick or gravel. The soil's pH reaction should be about 6. Feeding is desirable about once in two weeks between March and August, using a fertiliser containing extra potash and phosphate.

Cacti are propagated from seeds, cuttings, offshoots or grafts, but professional knowledge and practical experience are required to succeed at this.

Cacti can be stood directly on windowsills or in flower windows glassed-in on one side. For a more numerous collection of cacti you will need a greenhouse on the south-east or south-facing side of the house.

2

Astrophytum ornatum, the Star Cactus or Bishop's Cap (1) belongs to the lime-loving cacti. It has spines 2−4 cm (^{3}/4 − 1 ^{1}/2 in) long and wavy hairs on ribs. Various species of this genus are very popular as well, e.g. *A. asterias, A. coahuilense, A. senile.* In spring and autumn months watering should be limited, otherwise the vegetative period is prolonged. The astrophytums need a longer vegetative rest than the less demanding cacti.

Opuntia microdasys (2), the Prickly Pear or Bunny's Ears, has flattened and oblong joints. It is grown in sandy soil and over-winters in a completely dry environment. This species is propagated by cuttings, the basal parts of which should be desinfected and inserted in a

1

mixture of sand and peat where they
readily root. The compost should be
only slightly moist. Excessive watering
and lack of fresh air cause root rot.

Caladium
Araceae
Caladium bicolor

Almost 20 species of the Caladium genus grow in the tropical forests of South America. *Caladium bicolor* (1) has dark green heart-shaped leaves with white, yellow, pink or pale red variegation. This plant has given rise to many crosses which resulted in a number of hybrids. Though caladiums are among the most attractive plants as regards foliage colouring, they are not very important in gardening — probably because of their cultural requirements, particularly their exceptionally high demands for atmospheric moisture.

They are propagated by division of the large tubers (2) at sprouting time. They are set in 9 cm (3½ in) pots in March, on greenhouse staging in a peaty compost with a temperature of about 20−24 °C (68−75 °F). To start with the plants should be carefully watered and syringed. It is important to keep a high air humidity. Once two or three leaves have formed, the plants can be repotted into larger pots.

Prepare the growing medium from equal parts of leafmould blended with soil-based compost and peat at a pH of 5.0. These plants will not stand direct sun, so they should be grown slightly shaded at a constantly high temperature. From September, watering should be at a minimum and stopped altogether in mid-October. After the foliage has dried off, the tubers are left to over-winter in a pot at a temperature of about 18 °C (64 °F) in a dry place.

Caladiums should be fed from April to August with a compound fertiliser, preferably every 10 days.

3

Caladium hortulanum 'Triomphe de l'Exposition' (3) has broadly sagittate blue-green leaves with red variegation. In summer, caladium hybrids can be grown exclusively in closed winter gardens, flower windows and glass plant-cases. In rooms where the air is dry, caladiums often suffer from withering foliage.

Their flowers are inconspicuous. If pollinated, they form viable seeds which should be sown on the surface of a fine soil compost. Young, rather variable seedlings require very careful attention. Mist over the foliage daily with soft water at a temperature of 22−24 °C (72−75 °F) left to stand overnight.

2

1

65

Calathea, Peacock Plant
Calathea makoyana

Marantaceae

Over 100 species of Calathea can be found in Central and South America. The striking coloration of their foliage places them among the most attractive evergreen tropical plants. Calatheas are particularly suitable for flower windows and closed glass plant cases.

The Peacock plant, *Calathea makoyana* (1), is a native of Brazil. It can reach a height of 50—60 cm (20—24 in) indoors. Its broad leaves are dark green on the surface with a dark green elongated pattern along the veins. The underside of the leaf blades is red to brown-violet with conspicuous darker-coloured markings. The flowers are insignificant.

Calathea is propagated by division from February to May in a greenhouse with a high air humidity and a temperature of 25—28 °C (77—82 °F). Young plants need heavy shading, while older ones should be grown in semi-shade at temperatures of 22–24 °C (72–75 °F). The Peacock Plant should never be watered with cold water.

Young calatheas are potted in a mixture of 1 part coarse leafmould, 1 part peat and ⅕th part sand at pH 5.0—6.5. A dash of hoof and horn meal can be added. Supplementary feeding should be done carefully every two weeks, using a compound fertiliser solution. In dry conditions the foliage can be infested by red spider mites and suffer from dried off leaf tips.

The Zebra Plant, *Calathea zebrina* (2) is more robust. In favourable conditions, its leaves can reach a length of 1 m (3.3 ft).

Other species, such as *C. lancifolia,* the Rattlesnake Plant (3), as well as *C. lietzei* are sometimes offered by modern garden centres.

The indoor cultivation of calatheas is rather complex and demands great care.

2   3

These plants do best in high
temperatures and high air humidity
during spring and summer months. They
are only suitable for seasonal decoration
in centrally-heated rooms.

1

Calceolaria, Slipper Flower, Slipperwort

Scrophulariaceae

Calceolaria hybrids

Calceolarias native to the mountains of South America serve as the base for horticultural varieties which are the result of much hybridising. Horticulture makes use of interspecific hybrids, distinguished from each other by their different heights as well as flower size. They are marketed as Calceolaria hybrids (1). They form yellow, red, red-brown and yellow-brown blossoms (2, 3, 4).

The aim of contemporary plant breeding is a compact inflorescence with a large number of brightly coloured flowers, as well as early flowering and increased resistance to pests and diseases. Calceolarias last for only a limited time indoors, so they are considered as seasonal or gift plants. These plants dislike heat and thrive at 10−12 °C (50−54 °F). A suitable level of air humidity is achieved by regular ventilation.

Calceolarias are propagated exclusively from seeds in nurseries. They do best in medium to light soil mixtures, such as equal parts of soil-based compost and peat at a pH of 5.5−6.0. Calceolarias should be watered carefully, so the compost is permanently moist but never waterlogged. Plants which survive for more than a year need plenty of light, particularly in winter, while young ones should be slightly shaded.

Calceolarias grown indoors do not need feeding. As they are biennials, there is no reason to continue growing them after they have finished flowering.

C. integrifolia varieties can be planted out in gardens or grouped in tubs and bowls. They form low shrubby plants with small yellow flowers, which open in succession throughout the summer.

3

2

4

Calceolarias were among the most
widely cultivated indoor plants during the
last century up to the early 1950's. They
are now used only for seasonal
decoration of cool humid places indoors,
such as entrance halls, corridors and
heated winter gardens. Calceolarias are
also suitable for decorating floral tubs
and for grouping in ceramic bowls. They
are often attacked by aphids.

1

Campanula
Campanula isophylla

Campanulaceae

Campanula isophylla came originally from the mountains of southern Europe. It is a perennial plant with trailing stems and round leaves with toothed margins (3). The cultivar 'Alba' (1) has white flowers, while 'Mayi' (2) bears blue-coloured flowers and soft felty leaves. The flowers smother the plant from June to September.

Campanula winters at 5—12 °C (41—54 °F) with minimum watering. It is a light-lover and only young plants and newly sprouting ones need some shade. During the summer they are grown in full sun after being accustomed to it. Permanent intense heat causes wilting of the foliage and leaf fall.

The potting compost should be porous and medium heavy, such as an equal parts mix of peat, soil-based compost or loam and sand at a pH of 6.0—6.5.

Campanulas need frequent watering in summer. Though they will stand dry air, frequent ventilation is necessary. Minimum watering to stop the soil becoming dust dry is sufficient in winter. Excess water and high winter temperatures result in weak and premature growth. Supplementary feeding is best done with a solution of compound fertiliser from March to August.

Indoors, campanulas can be propagated by dividing mature plants or from cuttings. The best time for propagation is as growth begins. Cuttings root easily at 10—15 °C (50—59 °F). From three to five rooted cuttings can be set together in a single pot.

Combining blue and white campanulas can create a most impressive display. The plants repay the gardener's care with a continuing flood of small flowers.

C. isophylla is suitable for decorating windows, terraces, balconies, glassed-in passageways and staircases. It is especially decorative when potted in 20—30 cm (8—12 in) bowls and grown hanging on a wall or from the ceiling.

Plants grown in good-sized containers should be repotted once in 2—3 years during the spring. Change the surface layer of compost, about 3 cm (1¼ in) deep, every year.

2

1

3

Red Pepper
Capsicum annuum

The ornamental pepper is cultivated for its beautiful, long-lasting edible fruits. The *C. annuum* species (1) comes from South and Central America. Since they were brought to Europe by the Spaniards, peppers have been continually crossed and hybridised. Recent varieties have compact growth and branch well, bearing fruits of various shapes and coloured white, yellow or green as well as red, orange and deep violet (2, 3).

Peppers are easily propagated from seed, which should be sown in a medium light sandy soil between January and March. To start with they should be grown at about 20 °C (68 °F). Later 16 – 18 °C (61 – 64 °F) is sufficient. From the end of May plants can be set out in frames or in the garden. Before frosts arrive in autumn, peppers should be brought into a light, well-ventilated room, where they can ripen at 12 – 14 °C (54 – 57 °F).

Peppers need a soil-based compost mixed with sand with a pH from 6.0 to 6.5. While they are growing strongly the compost should be well moistened, but not waterlogged or the roots could rot. Peppers should be given as much light and air as possible while they are growing, particularly after the first repotting. They should be fed at two week intervals from April to October, with a solution of compound fertiliser. In late summer the proportion of potash should be increased and the water supply somewhat reduced.

2

Peppers thrive when placed in direct sunlight near a window. The fruits decorate the plants for several months. Pepper plants are usually on sale from October to December. At this time of year they should be stood on gravel trays to ensure humid air around them. Dry air in centrally heated homes can cause the fruits to wither.

Branches cut off and dried while

bearing ripe fruits can enhance the decor
even in places where the plant cannot be
grown in the winter because of the poor
light.

1

3

Ceropegia, String of Hearts
Ceropegia woodii

Asclepiadaceae

Ceropegias are succulents from South Africa and Asia. Some species are upright, others twine round branches or trail downwards. *C. woodii* (1) is the most widespread species. Its hanging or twining stems bear tiny, ovate to heart-shaped succulent leaves, dark green with light-coloured marbling along the veins. The flowers (2) are inconspicuous and of a brown-violet colour. Stems, which grow quite quickly, reach about 1 m (3.3 ft) long. Ceropegias are grown in winter temperatures from 14 to 16 °C (57−61 °F) preferably in partial shade.

This plant is propagated from cuttings from March to May. Five or six cuttings should be inserted in a 6−7 cm (2½−3 in) pot. When they have rooted through the pot, they can be repotted into shallow bowls. Ceropegias can also be propagated from stem tubers, which are easy to root. Any medium light porous soil will do, as for example, 2 parts of leafmould with 1 part of soil-based compost and a dash of sand at a pH of 5.5−6.5.

Watering should be cut down in winter, but more frequent watering is necessary while the plant is in active growth. Plants do well in a moderately humid atmosphere. Well-rooted plants can be fed at two-week intervals during the spring and summer. A liquid house plant fertiliser is most suitable. Mature plants should be placed as close to a window as possible but sheltered from direct sunlight so the young leaves are not scorched in early spring.

2

C. woodii ssp. *debilis* has narrow linear leaves with shallow wrinkling on both sides. It is similar in size to the previous species. Ceropegias do quite well in indoor conditions. They are undemanding in all respects and rather long-lived, even if given only minimum attention. They are suitable for bowls and baskets and can be used in an arrangement of epiphytic plants on a branch or trunk.

Mature plants should be placed on shelves, flower tables or windowsills so there is sufficient space for their long shoots to trail and to show off their characteristic habit of growth.

1

Chamaedorea, Dwarf Mountain Palm, Parlour Palm
Palmae

Chamaedorea elegans

Several dozen species of these small palms grow in the tropical mountains of Central and South America. *C. elegans* (1) is the most widely cultivated species. Its pinnate leaves grow in spirals on a short trunk. The broadly lanceolate leaflets are dark green. Each year from the age of three years, a lovely, yellow-orange inflorescence (3) appears, but the small globular flowers (4) soon drop off in indoor conditions. Older plants can reach a height of 100−150 cm (3 ft 3 in − 5 ft) in conservatories and some homes. The plant grows quite rapidly. When planted in the open soil, chamaedorea produces offshoots suitable for propagation. But sowing imported seeds (2) is a much more effective form of propagation.

Chamaedorea adapts well to indoor temperatures. It can be grown in winter at 16−22 °C (61−72 °F), even at some distance from the window. It should be protected from direct sunlight.

A suitable compost for repotting is made by mixing 2 parts leaf-mould, 2 parts medium heavy loam and 1 part peat. A pH of 5.5−6.5 will do. This plant needs repotting when pot-bound, early in spring. Water chamaedorea enough to moisten the root ball and to prevent the soil from drying out. Older plants should be watered less generously from November to February, as large amounts of water during this period could damage the roots and turn the foliage yellow.

Supplementary feeding is best done with a solution of compound fertiliser with a higher proportion of nitrogen during the period of vigorous growth from April to August.

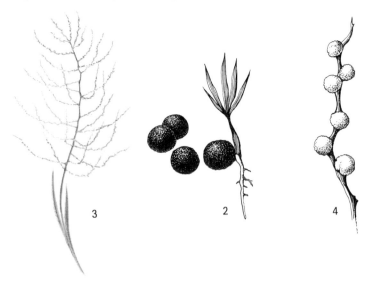

3   2   4

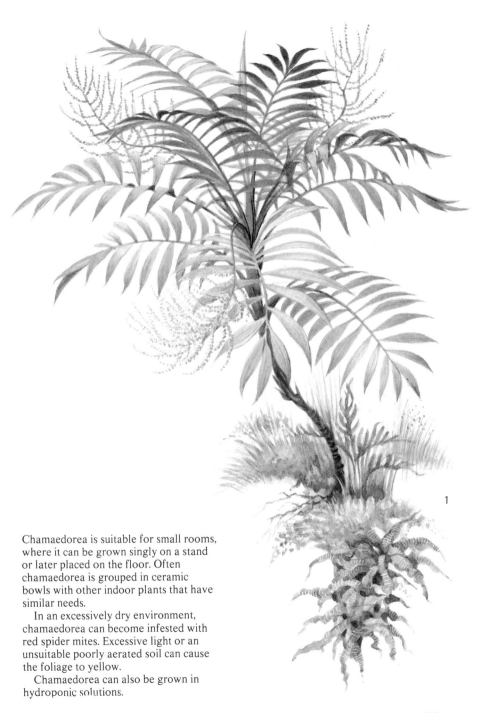

1

Chamaedorea is suitable for small rooms,
where it can be grown singly on a stand
or later placed on the floor. Often
chamaedorea is grouped in ceramic
bowls with other indoor plants that have
similar needs.

In an excessively dry environment,
chamaedorea can become infested with
red spider mites. Excessive light or an
unsuitable poorly aerated soil can cause
the foliage to yellow.

Chamaedorea can also be grown in
hydroponic solutions.

Chamaerops, European Fan Palm
Chamaerops humilis

Palmae

Chamaerops, the only European palm, grows in Greece, southern Italy and Spain, but can also be found in North Africa. Older plants have a short trunk branched at the base, bearing the remains of the leaf stalks covered in brown fibres. The leaves are fan-shaped, with spines along their stems. This palm produces profuse panicles of yellow flowers, followed by red fruits, which turn bluish black when ripe. This palm grows about 150 cm (5 ft) high.

Chamaerops humilis (1) is propagated from seed in nurseries. When a large palm is repotted in spring, several rooted offshoots can often be detached from its trunk. They root in a temperature of 18−20 °C (64−68 °F) in high humidity. Chamaerops winters in indoor temperatures from 5−15 °C (41−59 °F). In high winter temperatures, in dry, centrally-heated homes, the foliage turns yellow, dries off and is likely to be infested with pests. Chamaerops needs as much light as possible in winter and plenty of fresh air. It grows in full sun or in semi-shade in summer.

While growing vigorously, chamaerops needs regular watering, though it will tolerate an occasional shortage of water. It is grown in a mixture of 3 parts soil-based potting compost and 1 part sand at a pH of 6.0−7.0. The plant should be fed from February to October with a compound fertiliser solution. Repotting is recommended every two years from March to June, at first into clay pots, later into wooden containers.

2

Chamaerops is suitable for decoration of good-sized cool rooms, corridors, entrance spaces, winter gardens and palm houses. It can be grown outdoors from spring to autumn on terraces or balconies. Chamaerops can form a focal point in the design of a classical flower garden.
Trachycarpus fortunei (2) is often

78

1

referred to as *Chamaerops excelsa*. This palm has the same long life as *C. humilis* and bears leaves of similar shape. It grows taller than *C. humilis* and its trunk is never branched at the bottom. It is native to China. This palm has the same range of uses as *C. humilis*, but it is less important as an indoor plant.

Chlorophytum, Spider Plant   Liliaceae
Chlorophytum comosum 'Variegatum'

The green-leaved *C. comosum* was brought to Europe as early as the mid-19th century, but now the 'Variegatum' variety (1) is almost exclusively grown. Its narrow, grassy leaves, longitudinally striped with creamy white, grow in clumps, from which long, drooping flower stems and daughter plants spring. The plant flowers irregularly, the flowers being small and inconspicuous (2). Chlorophytum is one of the toughest of house plants. It can stand full sunshine once adapted to it, but also thrives in partial shade. Poor light results in dull coloured foliage, however.

The Spider Plant is propagated either by dividing the clumps or from daughter plants (3), which should be potted in 6−7 cm (2^1/$_2$−3 in) pots. From March to August the plantlets root at a temperature of 16−20 °C (61−68 °F) in 3−4 weeks. Older plants are grown in winter temperatures of 8−12 °C (46−54 °F), as they also adapt well to lower temperatures. If winter temperatures rise to 20 °C (68 °F) and the level of air humidity falls, the leaf tips can dry out. Watering depends on the air temperature as well as the stage of growth and should certainly be reduced in winter.

Betweeen March and May chlorophytums need an annual repotting in a mix of 3 parts soil-based compost and 2 parts peat at a pH of 6.0−7.0. From March to August they benefit from feeding with a compound fertiliser solution, given once a week.

As its demands are so modest and it is easily propagated, chlorophytum stands high in the growers' favour. It is often seen in hanging baskets or bottle gardens. Being so adaptable the Spider Plant is often grouped in ceramic bowls or window boxes with various annuals or geraniums.

Chlorophytum even does quite well in a north-facing position. It can be grown successfuly in a hydroponic solution, either as a single plant or as part of a group of plants.

In parks, chlorophytum is often bedded out with other flowering plants. The plants should then be moved back into a greenhouse before the autumn frosts begin.

1

Chrysanthemum
Compositae
Chrysanthemum morifolium hybrids

All the pot-grown and cut chrysanthemum cultivars available now are of hybrid origin. Varieties are mostly derived from the species *C. indicum* and *C. morifolium,* both native to East Asia, China and Japan. In their original home chrysanthemums flower earlier, during the summer, when the sub-tropical days gradually become shorter. In Europe, in different light and climatic conditions, chrysanthemums used to be considered typical autumn plants. Thanks to more recent ways of growing them, particularly controlling daylength, it is now possible to produce dwarf pot-grown chrysanthemums all the year round. They flower in a wide range of shades of white, yellow, pink, violet and bronze (1, 2, 3).

Only plants with flowers that have already unfurled can be placed further from the window, in a higher temperature of 20−22 °C (68−72 °F). Plants with closed or partially open buds should be stood close to a window in a cool room. At a temperature of 10−12 °C (50−54 °F) lateral buds will open as well.

Regular watering is a must, though permanently waterlogged soil can cause root rot and yellowing and dropping leaves. It is recommended to stand the pot in a larger ornamental container and fill the gap between the two with moistened coarse peat to give the plant the humidity it desires. Plants should be given plenty of fresh air.

2

The recently bred varieties of pot chrysanthemum differ in form and colour and have a wide range of uses. Besides their traditional use for decorating graves, they are suitable for balconies, terraces, flower windows and tubs. They can be bedded out or grouped in large ceramic bowls in gardens and parks. Chrysanthemums are also arranged in social rooms, exhibition halls and foyers. Home gardeners can also group a number of chrysanthemums in bowls, along with ivies, tradescantias or cissus. Combining several colours makes a more impressive display.

How long chrysanthemums last
indoors depends on the variety as well as
the heat, light and relative air humidity. In
favourable conditions the flowers can last
up to 4—6 weeks.

1

3

Grape Ivy
Cissus rhombifolia 'Ellen Danica'

Vitaceae

Cissus rhombifolia (2) was brought to Europe from South Africa. At present the cultivar 'Ellen Danica' (1) fills an important place among trailing and pot-grown indoor plants. This plant is a climber with long-petioled, trifoliate leaves with coarsely dentate margins (3). They are dark green on the upper side and brown-green on the underside. Unlike the species itself, the cultivar can be grown at higher winter temperatures of about 16—20 °C (61—68 °F), so its range of uses is considerably greater. It should be sheltered from direct sun, as it requires diffused light or semi-shade.

It is best propagated between March and August from ripe stem or tip cuttings with one to three fully-developed leaves. Cuttings root well in 3 parts peat mixed with 1 part sand with bottom heat to lift the temperature of the compost. It is best to set three to five cuttings in a small pot (5–7 cm/2–3 in). When they have rooted, the plants should be potted into a 10 cm (4 in) pot, adding 1 part of soil-based compost to the original mixture. The ideal pH value for the mixture is about 5.5—7.5.

Water liberally at higher temperatures and carefully mist the foliage in the morning only. Supplementary feeding is desirable from March to September with a compound fertiliser solution containing extra nitrogen. In excessively dry air, red spider mites sometimes appear on the undersides of the leaves, and aphids at the base of the petioles.

2

The cultivar 'Ellen Danica' is also suitable for hydroponic cultivation.

The Kangaroo Vine, *Cissus antarctica,* is a rewarding plant for cool rooms and verandas, but it cannot tolerate dry air and temperatures over 16 °C (61 °F) in winter.

The Begonia Vine, *Cissus discolor,* comes from Java. It has velvety violet, pointed leaves with a silvery grey pattern. It is highly ornamental, but is apt to shed its leaves if winter temperatures fall too low. In centrally-heated homes it suffers from the dry atmosphere. It is occasionally planted in winter gardens, flower windows and glazed plant cases.

Never expose cissus foliage to very humid air when temperatures are low in winter.

1

3

85

Mandarin, Tangerine
Citrus reticulata

Citrus are grown for their fruit in all sub-tropical regions of the world. *Citrus reticulata* (1) has narrow leathery leaves (2) and fragrant, purplish white flowers (3).

The long-term cultivation of fruit-bearing citrus is rather demanding in indoor conditions. It is best to buy plants in flower at a nursery, for the lovely plants with dense foliage grown from the seeds of purchased fruits often do not flower.

When they are in active growth they need a temperature of 16−18 °C (61−64 °F). Citrus dislike soil temperatures higher than 25 °C (77 °F). Whenever the temperature rises above 30 °C (86 °F) the necessary extra air humidity is provided by frequent misting and by evaporation of water from bowls. The ideal winter temperature ranges from 6−10 °C (43−50 °F). Citrus can be grown in direct sun — they need really good light. Water regularly with unchlorinated water during the growing season, though excessively damp soil can be more harmful than slightly dried out compost. Plants need restrained watering in winter. February to March is the best time for repotting. Do not remove the old soil from the root ball. The soil mixture should be slightly acid, with a pH of 6.0−6.5, such as a mix of old leafmould, peat, loam and sand.

Citruses should be fed with a 0.2% solution of compound fertiliser once a week from March to October.

By the end of May, plants can be moved to a sunny position in the garden or on a balcony or terrace. Pots can be plunged in the ground or stood inside a large container with permanently moist peat packed between the two containers. In winter, keep tangerines in well-lit, cool rooms.

Scale insects are liable to attack citrus. They are found on the undersides of the leaves.

3

2

1

Clerodendrum, Bleeding Heart Vine, Glory Bower
Clerodendrum thomsoniae

Verbenaceae

Clerodendrum thomsoniae (1) was brought to Europe from West Africa. It is an evergreen climber; the twining shoots reach a length of 2−4 m (6−12 ft). They bear conspicuous bicoloured flowers arranged in racemes. The calyx is white, the bright red petals later turn violet.

Clerodendron is propagated in February to April from stem cuttings, either woody or soft, three to five of which should be inserted in a 7 cm (2½ in) pot filled with a mix of peat and sand. The rooted cuttings should be transplanted into 10−11 cm (4−4½ in) pots of 2 parts leafmould, 2 parts peat and 1 part sand at a pH of 5.5−6.5. Rooting and young plants should be kept shaded from the hottest sun at a temperature of 20−22 °C (68−72 °F). Clerodendrum needs regular watering during its growing season. The necessary air humidity is provided by misting. Side shoots should be pruned to strengthen the plants and keep them compact.

Clerodendrums require feeding at 7−10 day intervals from February to October. It is best to use a compound fertiliser. The plants should be gradually given more light and hardened off by ventilation and a reduction in temperature. At the end of September, when clerodendrums finish flowering, watering should be gradually cut down. Move the plants into a room at a temperature of 5−12 °C (41−54 °F) for the winter, when they enjoy as much air and light as possible. Keep compost only slightly moist. Prune the sideshoots in mid-February.

2

C. hastatum with white petals and purple sepals is sometimes seen in cultivation, as well as the Java Glorybean, *C. speciosissimum* (2), with red flowers. Both species are of East Asian origin. Their cultural requirements are similar to those of *C. thomsoniae*.

Clerodenrums are used for the indoor decoration of windows, glassed-in verandas, staircases and halls. Two to four plants in a large pot can be supported with a cane or grown near a wooden trellis. They can also be stood

on shelves to trail downwards. As they
demand special conditions, it is not
advisable to group clerodendrums with
other plants.

Clivia, Kaffir Lily
Clivia miniata

Amaryllidaceae

In the first half of this century, clivias ranked among the most popular house plants. The reason they have lost much of their popularity is that plants propagated from seed take 4—6 years to start flowering.

C. miniata (1) from South Africa is the most widely seen species in cultivation at present. This species has dark green strap-like leaves up to 50 cm (20 in) long. The leaves spring up in tufts from the fleshy roots. Conspicuous clusters of scarlet or yellow-orange flowers (2) are borne on thick stalks up to 60 cm (2 ft) high. After the flowers fall, clivia is decorated with orange-red fruits (3). Indoors, the plant is propagated by dividing the large clumps after it has finished flowering. Be careful not to damage its roots when doing this. The most suitable potting mixture consists of 2 parts old leafmould to 1 part loam (or compost) and 1 part peat with a pH value of about 6.

Every 2—4 years clivias are moved into slightly larger pots. If this is not done, flowering deteriorates. Spring is their natural flowering season, but some strong adult plants can flower in autumn as well. Flowering can be encouraged by reducing the water supply from August to September. Afterwards, water regularly according to the room temperature. Grow clivias in a winter temperature of 2—15 °C (54—59 °F). They are quite tolerant of fluctuating temperatures too. They grow well in diffused light and in summer a little sun is desirable. Clivias should be fed from March to August with a liquid fertiliser containing extra phosphate.

3

Clivias were much hybridised in the past. The yellow-flowered C. miniata 'Citrina' and the more robust C. miniata 'Robusta' with larger flowers are among the most valued varieties.

C. nobilis bears about 40—50 vermilion flowers on a single stalk but is rarely seen in cultivation.

Clivias are very long-lived plants when grown indoors. They can be stood quite a distance from a window and withstand dry air and fumes. They are suitable for decorating corridors, halls, offices and workrooms. In summer clivias can stand

out on balconies or in a sheltered
position in the garden. Until hardened off,
the plants can be damaged by excessive
sunlight.

1

2

Croton, Joseph's Coat
Codiaeum variegatum

Euphorbiaceae

The crotons, native to Indonesia and the Pacific Islands, gave rise to the *Codiaeum variegatum* hybrids (1), which are quite important to indoor gardening. The hybrids have multi-coloured leaves which often vary greatly in shape (2, 3, 4). Most appreciated are the broad-leaved cultivars with entire or lobed leaves. The flowers are inconspicuous. In indoor conditions, crotons grow about 100—150 cm (39—60 in) high.

Crotons are propagated from tip cuttings between February and October. The cuttings root in 7 cm (3 in) pots, inserted in a mix of 2 parts sand and 1 part peat at an air temperature of 25—30 °C (77—86 °F) and high air humidity (90%). After the plants have been potted into larger pots, they are grown at 22—24 °C (72—75 °F) in 1 part leafmould and 1 part peat with a pH of 5.0—6.0 or in peat-based potting compost.

Repotting is done annually between March and mid-September. As insufficient light results in poor leaf coloration, crotons should be stood as close to a window as possible, after being accustomed to it gradually. Where light is poor all the time, crotons are apt to shed their leaves and even die. Low atmospheric moisture and excessive air circulation are equally harmful. The plants are also vulnerable to long periods of temperatures below 18 °C (64 °F).

They should be fed from mid-February to mid-October with a solution of compound fertiliser. Crotons require regular watering.

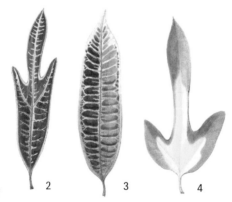

2   3   4

Despite their difficult demands and rather limited life in centrally-heated homes, crotons are among the most widespread indoor plants. They can be carefully placed as specimen plants or grouped together with other plants with similar requirements. Some cultivars can be grown in hydroponic solutions as well. But for the most part crotons tend to lose their ornamental qualities in the unfavourable growing conditions in our modern homes.

1

The commonest pests infesting crotons are red spider mites, scale insects and tarsonemid mites. In low winter temperatures, blotches of fungal origin may appear on the foliage from time to time.

93

Coleus, Flame Nettle
Coleus blumei hybrids

Labiatae

Over 150 species of Coleus grow in the tropics of Africa and Asia. They gave rise to the hybrids (1), which are important indoor plants. All the cultivars grown in nurseries nowadays are of hybrid origin.

Their soft leaves of various shapes and colours (2, 3, 4) are borne on the square stems. Coleus flowers from June to September with inconspicuous blue-white blossoms.

Propagation is easy from tip cuttings from January to May. They are inserted in small pots filled with equal parts of peat and sand. After the cuttings have rooted at a temperature of 20−22 °C (68−72 °F), they should be moved into larger pots in a mix of 1 part soil-based compost and ½ part sand at a pH of 5.5−6.5. Older plants can be grown at a temperature of 16−18 °C (61−64 °F). Coleus are easy to winter in a light position at a temperature of 12−15 °C (54−59 °F).

Coleus should be repotted in March or April to produce fully developed, colourful plants by the end of May. They are light-lovers and do well in full sun once they have been hardened to it. They should be watered regularly while in active growth but moderately in winter. Frequent ventilation is desirable. Cultivars with small leaves can be shaped by trimming, but the broad-leaved ones are usually grown untrimmed.

In rooms where the atmosphere is dry coleus are liable to be troubled by red spider mites. Sometimes whitefly appear on the undersides of the leaves. A compound fertiliser solution should be given from April to September.

Coleus is not a typical indoor plant. It is best suited for decorating windowsills and balconies as well as verandas outdoors. It is often bedded out, along with annuals and other matching plants. Before the onset of the first autumn frosts, coleus should be moved into a room or conservatory to overwinter.

2

3

4

Do not start planting out before late May, as an extended fall in temperature below freezing will kill the plants.

Though coleus can be grown successfully in hydroponic containers, young stock should be kept ready to replace older plants, which tend to lose their beauty after a year's growth.

95

Columnea, Goldfish Plant
Columnea gloriosa

Gesneriaceae

Over a hundred species of these demanding plants can be found in the tropics of South and Central America. The hybrids are of particular interest to the house plant enthusiast, as they are more resilient and flower more profusely than the original species. Most widely encountered is *C. gloriosa* (1). It generally forms a subshrubby plant clothed with small, ovate to lanceolate leaves, which are dark green with a touch of brown. The bright red flowers are about 5−7 cm (2−3 in) long (2).

Stem cuttings should be taken from February to May and five or seven inserted in a 7 cm (3 in) pot filled with 2 parts peat and 1 part sand. A temperature of 20−22 °C (68−72 °F) with deep shade and high air humidity are needed in the propagator. When rooted, cuttings should be potted into larger pots, in a mix of 2 parts half-decomposed leafmould, 2 parts peat and 1 part sand at a pH of 5.5−6.5. The sprouting side shoots require plenty of air and space. They should be carefully protected from direct sunlight, though insufficient light results in poor flowering. Flower formation is encouraged by a drop in temperature to 12−15 °C (54−59 °F). During this period, watering should be kept to a minimum and fertiliser should be withheld completely. After good-sized buds have developed, the temperature should again be increased to 20 °C (68 °F). A compound fertiliser solution should be given from February to October.

Among other species of some importance, *C. banksii* with large striking flowers should be mentioned, as well as small-leaved *C. hirta* (3). They are grown in hanging bowls, baskets or pots.

Columneas are suitable for decorating closed flower windows and glass plant cases. They don't thrive in rooms where the air is dry and tend to lose their leaves rapidly. These plants are rather sensitive to changes of surroundings, particularly at flowering time.

2

3

1

Cordyline, Cabbage Palm
Cordyline terminalis

Agavaceae

The heat-loving cordylines are native to India, Malaysia and Polynesia, while the cold-loving ones come from north-east Australia and New Zealand. The most suitable for indoor cultivation are the variegated cultivars of *Cordyline terminalis* (1). They reach a height of 30−100 cm (12−40 in). Long-petioled leaves are borne on the slender stem. Their basic green colouring is often offset by stripes of irregular shape and arrangement, in orange, red or violet. This heat-lover needs winter temperatures of 18−24 °C (64−75 °F) and sufficient light, though it should be protected from direct sunlight. The plant does well in an equal parts mix of peat, leafmould and soil-based compost at a pH of 5.5−6.5.

The plants should be moved into larger pots between April and August to avoid the root ball becoming too dry. Water the plants freely in summer but little in winter. High air humidity must be provided, otherwise the leaf tips dry out and the leaves may fall. Cordylines benefit from feeding from February to November with a solution of compound fertiliser. Excess nitrogen results in poorly coloured foliage.

Propagation of cordylines is rather complicated. Taking tip or stem cuttings has proved the best method of propagation, the cuttings being inserted in a mixture of equal parts peat and sand. In a dry atmosphere cordylines can be infested by red spider mites and occasionally by thrips.

In the wild, cordylines grow as shrubs, reaching a height of several metres (2).

3

Due to this species' special demands, however, it is only of limited use for indoor cultivation.

Besides the heat-loving cordylines, the narrow-leaved species are grown in a limited quantity, such as the New Zealand Cabbage Tree, also called the Grass Palm, *Cordyline australis* (3), as well as *C. indivisa.* They thrive in soil-based compost and do not require high winter temperatures, being content at 8−12 °C (46−45 °F). They are suitable for decorating terraces, patios and balconies in summer. Unlike *C. terminalis,* these plants have a long life.

Hydroponic cultivation of cordylines is limited, as the variegated cultivars often dry out and drop their leaves.

Cryptanthus, Zebra Plant
Bromeliaceae
Cryptanthus zonatus var. *fuscus*

Cryptanthus zonatus var. *fuscus* (1), a native of Brazil, is not notable for its flowers, but is remarkable for the unusual coloration of its stiff, pointed leaves arranged in smallish rosettes. This plant lives happily for a long time in centrally heated rooms. It is used to decorate flower windows and glass plant cases as well as trunks covered in epiphytic plants, though it can be grown in bowls with other plants.

C. zonatus has leaves 15—25 cm (6—10 in) long, with silvery grey transverse stripes, slightly wavy on the margins. It is propagated by removing and potting up the daughter plants between March and August. These offsets are potted in 6 cm (2½ in) pots filled with coarse peat to which polystyrene flakes have been added. They root at about 24 °C (75 °F). Older plants are grown in 8—10 cm (3—4 in) pots in an equal parts mix of chopped bark and peat at a pH value of 4.5—5.5. The potting compost is made more porous and better aerated by adding perlite.

Cryptanthus should be watered only with soft water, which should not be too cold during the winter. Frequent misting is desirable during the summer. Plants should be grown in slight shade, as they will only tolerate direct sunlight for short periods. Their colouring is, however, rather bright. Supplementary feeding is necessary once a month from March to October, with a solution of compound fertiliser.

2

Other species are also grown, including *C. fosterianus,* the Pheasant Leaf (2), as well as *C. bivittatus* (3), *C. roseus, C. bromelioides,* the Rainbow Star, and many others.

Cryptanthus are highly resistant to pests and diseases. Sometimes, the leaf tips dry out and in soft-leaved species considerable areas can be damaged. This is generally caused by underwatering, dry air or overfeeding. Greenhouse plants can be damaged by direct sunlight if not accustomed to it gradually.

The lovely coloured leaf rosettes are used in wedding bouquets, flower baskets and other decorative arrangements.

Cyclamen, Sow Bread
Cyclamen persicum

Primulaceae

C. persicum (1) grows in the wild in the Eastern Mediterranean area. It has played the major role, along with other species, in the development of the modern cyclamen cultivars. Their quality has been continually improved by breeding during the several hundred years they have been grown. This has been focused on the size as well as the number of flowers, different flower forms and colours (2, 3) and early flowering.

The round leaves, often marbled with white, silver or grey, spring from an underground tuber. The flower colours range from white through various shades of pink to red or violet. The cyclamen is not a permanent house plant. It is grown in nurseries and marketed from August to May.

When grown indoors, cyclamen should be placed as close to a window as possible. A constant temperature of 10−15 °C (50−59 °F) as well as high air humidity should be provided. At temperatures below 10 °C (50 °F) the plants will continue flowering happily for several months. Cyclamen are harmed by dry atmospheres and heat. In these conditions they are likely to wilt rapidly, bud development ceases and their leaves turn yellow and fall.

Cyclamen require regular watering. The pots should be stood on flat trays and supplied with water according to their needs. It is important to keep water off the tuber or it could rot. Faded flowers should be pulled out complete with their stems, as any pieces of stem left behind can decay and infect the tuber with fungal diseases.

2   3

Given favourable conditions, it is worth trying to grow new flowering plants from tubers (4). Faded plants are left to dry, dead growth is removed and the tubers are then stored in a cool dry room until summer. In late summer pot the tubers in 12−14 cm (4½−5½ in) pots filled with a light mixture of 2 parts leafmould, 1 part peat and ½ part sand at a pH of 5.5−6.5. Add a complete slow-release granulated fertiliser or a dash of bone meal to the mixture.

The pots should be plunged in the ground in a garden frame, preferably in a slightly shaded spot. Regular watering is desirable, the shooting leaves requiring

4

1

a mist as often as several times a day.
During winter and spring cyclamen
grown in this way often flower much
more profusely than those grown from
seed.

Cyperus, Umbrella Grass
Cyperus alternifolius

Cyperaceae

Umbrella Grass, *Cyperus alternifolius* (1), is a native of Madagascar where it grows as a swamp plant. This plant can grow up to 120 cm (4 ft) indoors. Its blade-like stems, grouped in clumps, bear narrow, radially arranged, deep green leaves at the top. The inconspicuous flower cluster is a whitish green colour.

From March to June, cyperus can be propagated by dividing the clumps, or from leaf rosette cuttings, which root in moist sand or in clean soft water. Young rooted plants are potted three to a 10−11 cm (4−4½ in) pot filled with a mix of 2 parts peat, 1 part loam and ½ part sand at a pH 5.5−6.5. The pots should be placed in water for a third of their depth. Cyperus are grown in slight shade at a temperature of about 20 °C (68 °F) and moved into bigger pots from March to May. Older plants can stand a winter temperature of about 15 °C (59 °F).

Cyperus require feeding with a solution of compound fertiliser at fortnightly intervals from March to September. A nutrient solution can be poured straight into a container placed under the pot. Cyperus demand plenty of soft water while growing, preferably rain water or boiled water. They need slight shading, as excessive light will turn their leaves yellow. Cyperus often suffer from browning of the leaf tips. This can be caused by unsuitable chemical composition of water, dry air or a shortage of nutrients in the soil.

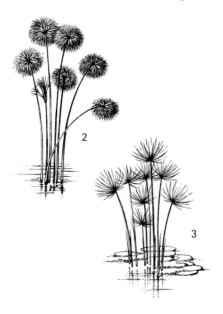

The robust *C. papyrus,* 2 m (6 ft 6 in) or more high, known as the Egyptian Paper Rush or Papyrus (2), can be grown in pools in large winter gardens, but the more delicate *C. haspan* (3) requires much less space for cultivation.

Cyperus are also suitable for aquaria, terraria and greenhouse pools. Any older leaves that turn yellow should be cut off promptly and the water in the containers in which they are grown should be changed, as decomposing organic residues in the water, could cause browning and dying of the leaf tips.

1

The stems of the smaller kinds of cyperus can serve as useful foliage when arranging cut flowers in vases or sticking them up in the Japanese needlepoint holders known as 'kenzans'.

Dieffenbachia, Dumb Cane
Dieffenbachia picta

Araceae

Dieffenbachias were brought to Europe at the end of the last century mostly from the tropical forests of Central and South America. Among 30 species described, *D. picta* and its cultivars, such as 'Exotica' (1) are of outstanding importance in horticulture. The upright stem bears oval to oblong lanceolate leaves, dark green with white or yellow variegation. The flowers (2) are interesting in shape, but inconspicuous in colour.

In summer, dieffenbachias thrive in semi-shade. Excessive light bleaches their leaves, so they lose their typical colouring, the plants turn yellow and the leaf tips dry out. On the other hand, insufficient light in winter results in soft stem growth and poor leaf colouring.

These plants need high air humidity. They dislike fluctuating temperatures as well as long periods at temperatures below 20 °C (68 °F). They grow best at 22−25 °C (72−77 °F), potted either in a peaty compost and leaf mould, or in a mix of 3 parts peat and 1 part loam. The pH should be adjusted to 5.0−5.5.

Dieffenbachias need repotting every year between March and August. As the plants transpire large amounts of water, they need frequent watering. Never water them with cold water. Supplementary feeding is done with a solution of compound fertiliser with a balanced ratio of nitrogen and potash from March to October.

Dieffenbachias are easily propagated from tip cuttings as well as from stem sections each with a single bud. They are quick to root in water, peat or light loam.

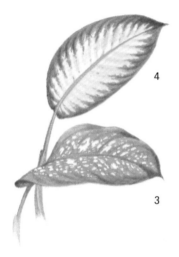

4

3

Among the cultivars of *D. picta* (3), 'Rudolph Roehrs' and 'Pia' are the most widely grown. *D. amoena* is another important species. Its cultivars 'Tropic White' (4) and 'Tropic Snow' have large spotted leaves and grow up to 120−150 cm (4−5 ft) indoors.

The bottom leaves of dieffenbachias often dry off, but there is no way of preventing this. Best results are achieved with dieffenbachias grown in flower windows and glass plant cases, where they can be provided with the extra air humidity they love. All species of dieffenbachia can be grown hydroponically.

Stem rot is the most dangerous disease
of dieffenbachias, encouraged by
overwatering and low temperatures. Dry
atmosphere quickly encourages
infestation with red spider mites.

107

Dizygotheca, False Aralia, Finger Aralia   Araliaceae
Dizygotheca elegantissima

Dizygotheca elegantissima (1), a native of New Caledonia, occasion-aly reaches a height of 2 metres (6 ft 6 in) indoors. In winter particu-larly it is likely to drop some of its leaves and therefore lose some of its undoubted beauty. Its narrow palmate leaves with toothed margins are olive-green in colour. The midribs, leaf margins and stems are all tinged a reddish colour. The plant has a generally airy habit and looks very decorative in a modern home. Its flowers are insignificant.

Dizygotheca is propagated from imported seeds in specialist nurse-ries. Indoor propagation from cuttings is usually a failure. This plant needs winter temperatures of 20−24 °C (68−75 °F), dislikes fluctu-ating temperatures and cold draughts, and central heating not fitted with air humidity regulators. Dizygotheca should be grown in diffused light or in slight shade. It needs repotting each year between March and May, preferably in a compost consisting of 2 parts coarse leaf-mould, 1 part loam or soil-based compost and 1 part peat at a pH of 5.5−6.5.

Dizygotheca requires regular watering, as it won't tolerate dried out soil. Maintain a high air humidity throughout the year. A solution of compound fertiliser should be applied with discretion at fortnightly intervals from March to September.

2

Owing to these plants' dislike of modern living conditions, particularly dry air, they are only of limited use. They can be planted in largish ceramic bowls with other plants that have bright-coloured flowers and are used for seasonal decoration. The cultivar 'Castor' makes compact columnar growth with shorter and broader leaves than the species itself (2).

Dizygothecas can be placed in the corners of flower windows and glass plant cases, backed up by the lower growth of other plants. Leaf fall is usually caused by inadequate attention to their needs for water, humidity and so on. Mealy bugs sometimes appear at the base

of the leaf stalks and on the undersides of old leaves.

Dizygothecas are also suitable for hydroponic cultivation in a slightly warm and dry environment, usually being grown as specimen plants.

1

Dracaena
Dracaena deremensis 'Warneckii'

Agavaceae

Dracaenas originating in tropical Africa are of considerable horticultural value. *D. deremensis* in particular has yielded a number of cultivars. Its long, sessile, lanceolate, arching olive-green leaves are borne on a woody stem. The leaves of most of the cultivars are longitudinally striped. In some cultivars, such as 'Warneckii' (1), shades of white predominate, while in 'Rhoersii' the prevailing colour is yellow.

Dracaenas are grown at winter temperatures of 20−22 °C (68−72 °F). An extended period of temperatures below 16 °C (61 °F) can upset its growth. In summer, plants should be placed in semishade further from a window, but in winter they should be moved closer to the window.

Dracaenas are potted in a mix of 3 parts peat and 2 parts loam or in 2 parts leafmould mixed with 1 part peat at a pH of 5.5−6.5. Young plants need repotting every year between April and August, but mature ones can be repotted every two years. Water the plants with water that has been left to stand overnight. The foliage benefits from misting, and the plants enjoy high air humidity.

Supplementary feeding is done from February to November, using a solution of compound fertiliser with a balanced ratio of nitrogen and potash. An excess of nitrogen results in poor leaf colouring.

Dracaenas are propagated from tip or stem cuttings. Insert the cuttings in 9−10 cm (3½−4 in) pots filled with a mix of equal parts peat and sand. The most damaging disease of these plants is leaf rot.

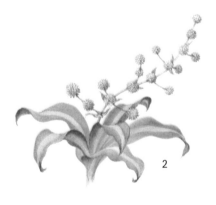

2

D. fragrans is a highly valued species with leaves 7−8 cm (2¾−3 in) wide and a more robust habit of growth. Its cultivars are also grown, among them 'Lindenii' striped yellow along the margins and 'Massangeana' (2) with a central yellow stripe. *D. surculosa* is a shrubby plant with ovate to elliptical, glossy green leaves with scattered yellow spots. *D. marginata* 'Tricolor' (3) has highly decorative, narrow lanceolate leaves. Mature dracaenas usually develop a trunk leafless at the base.

1

3

Scindapsus, Devil's Ivy, Golden Pothos
Epipremnum aureum
syn. *Scindapsus aureus*

Araceae

Epipremnum aureum, better known as *Scindapsus aureus* (1), a native of the Solomon Islands, is one of the most widely grown ornamental-leaved house plants. It climbs or trails. The heart-shaped yellow-variegated leaves are borne on slender stems. The side shoots grow up to 15 m (49 ft) long. Well-fed older plants can develop leaves of abnormal size, known as the old form of the leaves.

Scindapsus is easily propagated from stem cuttings, which root in a compost temperature of 24 − 26 °C (75 − 79 °F) and an air temperature of 22 − 24 °C (72 − 75 °F) in leafmould or peat mixed with sand. Five to seven cuttings are inserted in a 10 cm (4 in) pot and covered with plastic sheeting to start with. Scindapsus can be propagated all the year round.

Plants grown indoors are poorly coloured if grown in deep shade, so they should be kept in diffused light or partial shade at a temperature of 18 − 20 °C (64 − 68 °F) with maximum air humidity. The plants should be watered freely from February to October but cautiously in December and January. They grow well in a light soil mixture, such as 2 parts leafmould, 1 part peat and ½ part sand at a pH of 5.5 − 6.5. Plants should be repotted between March and August. Regular feeding is desirable at 10 − 14 day intervals, using a compound fertiliser.

3

The cultivar 'Marble Queen' (2) has a more delicate growth habit than the species itself. Its leaves have conspicuous white mottling.

Devil's Ivy is grown in hanging baskets or similar containers from which its shoots trail. The plant can also be attached to a moss-covered cane. When planted in a glass plant case or flower window the plant makes a lush growth so it should be given plenty of room. *Scindapsus pictus* (3) is native to Indonesia and the Philippine Islands. Its matt leathery leaves are patterned with silvery grey. As this plant demands rather high air humidity, flower windows and glass plant cases are the only suitable positions for its long-term cultivation. This plant does not grow as tall, but its cultivation and other requirements are the same as for Devil's Ivy.

1

2

Cape Heath
Erica gracilis

Ericaceae

Erica gracilis (1, 3), which came to us from the mountains of South Africa, is the most important heath species grown indoors. Heaths have small, stiff, needle-like leaves and tiny bell-shaped flowers in shades of red and pink. *E. gracilis* 'Alba' (2) has white blossoms.

Cape Heaths grow 25 – 40 cm (10 – 16 in) tall. They are not on sale in florists before August, as they are raised in specialist nurseries, where they are grown until they come into flower.

After the plant has been brought home from the florists, its pot should be plunged in water for 2 – 4 hours, as its root ball should never dry out. It should then be tipped out of its pot and planted in an ornamental container or bedded out, preferably in moist coarse peat and sand. After this, water the heath regularly with soft (non-limy) water. On hot days, the whole plant should be misted or sprayed. Dry air is usually the reason for the flower buds failing to open.

Heaths don't mind full sun but thrive in partial shade as well. They do not need feeding once they have finished growing.

If you wish to grow your heath again next year, you should over-winter it in a light room at a maximum temperature of 15 °C (59 °F) in high air humidity. In March, prune back the fresh sideshoots, increase the temperature and repot the plant. Give it a solution of compound fertiliser every 10 – 14 days to the end of August. After the end of May heath can be placed outdoors.

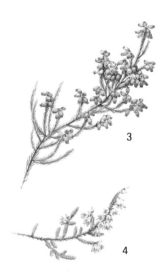

3

4

During the spring, the pink, pinkish red, pinkish orange and pinkish white Erica hybrids are in flower. They make more robust growth and their flowers are longer. At a temperature of 6 – 10 °C (43 – 50 °F) the hybrids can last indoors for several months.

E. carnea (4) is one of the dainty spring flowering heaths. These hard plants can be set in ceramic bowls and windowboxes.

Heaths are used for autumn potting in ceramic bowls and windowboxes and for decorating graves. They can also be grown with dwarf conifers and shrubs,

1

2

ornamental perennials or ivy. Containers
filled with potted heaths can be placed on
balconies or terraces, in windows as well
as out in the garden, where they can stay
until winter comes.

Euonymus, Japanese Spindle Tree   Celastraceae
Euonymus japonicus

Euonymus japonicus (1) is one of the most widely used plants for decorating rooms with winter temperature ranging from 0−10 °C (32−50 °F). This undemanding evergreen shrub is native to Japan and China, where it has long been grown in a variety of cultivars. It reaches a height of about 2 metres (6 ft 6 in). Its dark green branches bear leathery oval leaves, dark green in colour and glossy on the upper side. This shrub flowers in June and July with inconspicuous whitish flowers.

Euonymus is propagated between February and May or in late summer from tip cuttings. They root well when shaded in a semi-warm greenhouse or frame. The compost should not be too light. For pot-grown plants the most suitable is a mixture of 3 parts soil-based potting compost with 1 part peat and 1 part sand at a pH of 6.0−7.0.

From April to August, the shrubs should be fed with a solution of compound fertiliser. Regular watering is necessary as well as spraying with soft (non-limy) water on hot summer days. They should be given an airy position, as euonymus will not tolerate a hot, dry atmosphere. They can be placed in cool rooms, porches and staircases. From spring to autumn they can be placed outdoors to decorate house entrances, garden arbours and terraces.

2

Given favourable conditions, euonymus grow quite rapidly and need regular pruning back, particularly while they are in active growth. This produces a dense and compact mass of foliage on well-branched sideshoots. Even quite old shrubs stand up well to rejuvenation by careful pruning.

E. japonicus is found in cultivation not only in various forms with different sizes of leaves, but also in a number of variegated cultivars. The leaves of *E. japonicus* 'Albomarginatus' are spotted white, while 'Aureomarginatus' (2) has striking yellow leaf margins.

E. fortunei, var. *radicans* is a hardy prostrate species, suitable for clothing banks in the garden that are permanently in shade. This species winter well in cold, rather damp rooms, given sufficient light. In dry conditions it tends to shed its older leaves.

1

Poinsettia
Euphorbia pulcherrima

Euphorbiaceae

Poinsettia (1) comes from the tropics of Mexico and Central America. It is a shrubby plant clothed in long lanceolate, lobed, green leaves. Clusters of inconspicuous flowers form at the tops of the main branches, and close beneath them the rosettes of spectacularly coloured bracts. These can be red, reddish orange, pink, or greenish white (2, 3). The plant flowers from November to February.

Poinsettia is propagated from tip cuttings bearing 4−5 leaves between June and mid-September. Before they are inserted the cuttings should be dipped in tepid water to dissolve the milky sap that obstructs the tissues after it has dried. The cuttings should not be allowed to wilt. They root under plastic sheeting in small pots of an equal parts mix of leaf mould and peat at a temperature of 22−24 °C (72−75 °F) within about 3−4 weeks. Rooted cuttings should be potted in 10 cm (4 in) pots of the same mixture as the rooting medium, at a pH of 5.5−6.5.

Poinsettias are grown in full light, at a temperature of 20−22 °C (68−72 °F) up to flowering time, when the temperature should be reduced to 18−20 °C (64−68 °F). Fluctuating temperatures and draughts will cause them to drop their lower leaves. Indoors poinsettias should be watered frequently, but waterlogged roots are more harmful than a temporary shortage of water. They need feeding every week from July to November up to flowering time, with a solution of compound fertiliser containing extra nitrogen. After the bracts have faded, poinsettia plants can be used to provide fresh cuttings.

4

The Crown of Thorns, *E. milii* (4), is a rewarding and very tough euphorbia that flowers in winter. It tolerates dry air as well as a sunny position, but makes rather slow growth. This plant is happy in winter temperatures of 6−8 °C (43−46 °F). One part of soil-based potting compost and ½ part sand should be mixed to provide a suitable compost. *E. milii* is propagated from stem cuttings. Dip the cut surfaces in water for two hours and dry off before inserting them.

The Scarlet Plume, *E. fulgens,* has been grown for more than 100 years. It too

3

1

flowers during the winter, but it needs
a temperature of 20 – 22 °C (68 – 72 °F)
and a light spot. It should be protected
from direct sun. Withhold water from
March to April so the plant can rest for
a while. Older plants can be pruncd to
shape after they have shed their flowers.

2

119

Fatshedera, Ivy Tree, Fat-headed Lizzie
Fatshedera lizei

Araliaceae

The evergreen Fatshedera (1) was produced by hybridising *Fatsia japonica* and *Hedera helix hibernica,* plants of distinct genera. Its woody stem grows upright while young, but should later be supported with a cane or on trellis. The plant is clothed in three- to five-lobed glossy leaves and bears clusters of inconspicuous white flowers.

It is propagated from tip cuttings or from soft stem cuttings with two or three leaves. The cuttings root best in an air temperature of 18−20 °C (64−68 °F). When the cuttings have rooted in a medium light mixture, such as 1 part leaf mould and 1 part peat, they should be moved into larger pots and grown at a temperature of 12−15 °C (54−59 °F). Mature plants should be repotted in an equal part mix of leafmould, soil-based potting compost and peat at pH 4.5−5.5. Older plants should be placed in a light or semi-shaded position at a temperature of 5−10 °C (41−50 °F).

Watering should be generous and regular in summer, but in winter it should be considerably reduced. Fatshedera likes a higher air humidity than is normal in centrally-heated homes. It dislikes high air temperatures and dry air. It should be fed from March to September with a solution of compound fertiliser high in nitrogen. In a dry atmosphere the undersides of the leaves can sometimes be attacked by red spider mites and by less troublesome pests such as scale insects and tarsonemid mites.

2

Fatshedera lizei 'Variegata' (2) is a mutation of the hybrid. It has the same general habit and growth as *Fatshedera lizei,* but its leaves are variegated with white. It needs a similar environment and care.

Fatshedera usually grows successfully in a hydroponic solution. Provide it with the cool temperatures it prefers too.

1

In high temperatures and in dry air its
leaves turn yellow and drop off.
Fatshederas are suitable for
decorating moderately heated winter
gardens, halls and corridors.

Fatsia, Aralia, Castor Oil Plant
Fatsia japonica

Araliaceae

Fatsia japonica (1), which originated in Japan, used to rank among the most popular indoor plants. With the higher average winter temperature in our homes, however, and the simultaneous drop in air humidity, its usefulness became rather limited. It is a shrubby plant with large leathery, glossy, seven- to nine-lobed leaves.

Fatsias are propagated from seeds sown in nurseries between January and June. They germinate well in equal parts leafmould and peat without fertiliser at a temperature of 18−22 °C (64−68 °F) in high air humidity. Older plants and variegated forms are propagated from tip cuttings. Rooted plants are grown at a temperature of 12−15 °C (54−59 °F). Older plants overwinter at a temperature of 4−8 °C (39−46 °F) with a restricted water supply.

Fatsias should be shaded from intense sunshine, but deep shade produces long drawn growth which spoils their appearance. The plants are best repotted each year between March and September in a fertile compost with fertiliser added, such as an equal parts mix of soil-based potting compost and peat with a pH of 4.5−5.5.

Fatsias should be watered regularly and need much more water in summer than in winter. A solution of compound fertiliser with extra nitrogen should be given once a week from March to mid-September.

2

F. japonica 'Variegata' (2) is a mutant of this species whose leaves are variegated with white or yellow. Propagation by tip cuttings is usually rather difficult. This plant used to be propagated by grafting.

Fatsias are used to decorate cold airy rooms without any central heating, such as glassed-in verandas, staircases and moderately-heated winter gardens, where they can enjoy the conditions they need.

1

They are highly sensitive even to traces
of gas in the air, which turns their
leaves yellow. They then wilt and drop
off. Fatsias are troubled by the same pests
as fatshederas.

123

Ficus, Rubber Plant
Ficus elastica 'Decora'

Moraceae

Hundreds of species of Ficus are distributed in the tropics right round the world. *Ficus elastica* is native of India. It has broad elliptical, glossy, leathery leaves. The species gave rise to several highly esteemed cultivars, such as 'Decora' (1), 'Robusta' and the variegated cultivar 'Schrijweriana'.

Rubber plants are propagated throughout the year from tip cuttings with four or five leaves and one well-developed bud a piece. Dip the cuttings in tepid water to wash off the milky sap. They are inserted in a mix of equal parts peat and sand, their leaves bunched up round the stem with a rubber band, and covered with plastic sheet.

Indoors, rubber plant cuttings will root even in a glass of water. They need an air temperature of 26 — 30 °C (79 — 86 °F), but later the temperature can be reduced to 18 — 20 °C (64 — 68 °F) when rooted. Older plants will tolerate winter temperatures of about 15 °C (59 °F).

Rubber plants should be grown in a light position in winter. In summer they can stand full sun, once they have been accustomed to it. They need liberal watering and spraying during summer, but in winter the water supply and air humidity should be reduced.

Annual repotting is best done between March and August. Rubber plants do best in a humusy compost, such as 2 parts leafmould to 1 part peat at a pH of 5.5 — 6.5. For regular feeding from February to November, use a solution of compound fertiliser.

2

3

The small-leaved *F. benjamina* or
Weeping Fig (2) with several variegated
cultivars is another very important
species. It is a shrubby plant, content with
winter temperatures of 12−15 °C
(54−59 °F).

The Fiddle-leaf Fig, *F. lyrata,*
has large glossy, fiddle-shaped leaves, of
a mid-green colour. It is a tree species,
which branches when pruned. The
Climbing Fig, *F. pumila* (3), is a woody
climber with small leaves, varying in
shape. This plant is happy in winter
temperatures of 10−12 °C (50−54 °F),
but in a dry atmosphere it is apt to drop
its leaves.

1

125

Fittonia, Mosaic Plant, Painted Net Leaf Acanthaceae
Fittonia verschaffeltii

Fittonias come from South America. *F. verschaffeltii* (1) is a low, creeping, herbaceous plant with dark green oval leaves, decorated with a dense network of bright carmine veins. Its small, yellowish flowers are of no significance for decoration.

Fittonia is propagated from stem cuttings, usually between January and June. The cuttings will root without extra heat being given to the compost at about $22-26\ °C\ (72-79\ °F)$. Two or three cuttings can be inserted in a small pot filled with 2 parts peat and 1 part sand. Full-sized and older plants are grown in permanent shade at a temperature of $20-22\ °C\ (68-72\ °F)$. Fittonias will grow successfully even in deep shade, where other plants suffer from lack of light.

The plants should be repotted between March and May or in September or October. Prepare a compost from 2 parts well-rotted leaf-mould, 1 part peat, 1 part loam and $1/2$ part sand at a pH of $5-6$.

The plants need regular and ample watering during summer, but it should be reduced to a minimum in winter. Fittonias require high air humidity while they are growing, so frequent misting of the foliage is essential in summer. The plants are sensitive to draughts and fluctuating temperatures. Feed them from March to August with a compound fertiliser solution.

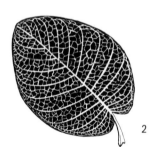

2

F. verschaffeltii 'Argyroneura' (2) has a profuse silvery white venation on its leaves. *F. gigantea* grows up to $50-60$ cm $(20-24$ in) high. This plant has reddish white felted stems and dark green leaves with carmine-red veins.

These plants do not live long indoors. They can only be grown successfully where the conditions match those of their natural habitat. High air humidity is the most important factor and can only be provided in air-conditioned glass plant-cases, flower windows and similar places, which are fairly small and almost entirely enclosed. Fittonias can occasionally be seen grouped with other plants in gift bowls, which are not intended for long-term cultivation.

1

Fuchsia, Lady's Ear-drop
Fuchsia hybrids

Onagraceae

Small-flowered hardy species of fuchsia can be found growing wild in the humid, airy cool mountain forests of Central and South America. There is great diversity of habit, adaptability, flower shape, size, fullness and colour (2, 3) among the many varieties (1) produced by generations of breeding.

Fuchsias are propagated between January and October from non-flowering tip cuttings with two or three pairs of leaves, obtained by cutting back the older plants. Insert the soft cuttings in 6 cm (2½ in) pots filled with an equal parts mix of peat and sand at a temperature of 18−22 °C (64−72 °F). Fuchsias propagated in spring should be gradually pruned to encourage them to branch well.

Young plants should be grown in slight shade at a temperature of 20−24 °C (68−75 °F). During the winter, the temperature should be reduced to 15−17 °C (59−63 °F). Older plants overwinter at a temperature of 5−10 °C (41−50 °F). Fuchsias have no liking for overheated air and should therefore be grown only in well-ventilated, rather humid rooms. They are grown in 10−12 cm (4−5 in) pots, in a loose rich compost, such as 1 part leafmould, 1 part loam and 2 parts peat at a pH of 5.5−6.5.

Older plants need repotting between February and August. After repotting and also during the winter, the plants should be watered cautiously, but while they are growing strongly they need watering frequently. Feed with a solution of compound fertiliser from February to September. Young plants need more nitrogen, but as they mature they demand more potash.

2

3

The various fuchsia cultivars are used according to their particular qualities. Low-growing cultivars with a compact habit, such as 'Cover Girl' and 'El Camino', are suitable for growing in pots, which can be placed out on shaded verandas, in corridors or on windowsills. Other cultivars like 'Swingtime' and 'Cascade' have a more pendulous habit, so they are grown in windowboxes, hanging baskets and ceramic bowls.

Fuchsia cordifolia (4), *F. microphylla* and other species were once grown too. They enjoyed the humid conditions in homes without central heating, particularly in country houses. Fuchsias in general won't stand long-term cultivation in modern homes where the air is dry.

129

Gloriosa, Glory Lily
Gloriosa rothschildiana

Liliaceae

A number of species of Gloriosa with attractive flowers can be found growing wild in Africa and tropical Asia. Among those grown as ornamentals, *G. rothschildiana* (1) is the most widely known. The cylindrical tubers formed on its underground rhizomes send up a climbing stem, which branches just above soil level. The stem bears leaves alternate or opposite. The flowers are dark red, sometimes bright red, with yellow margins to the petals.

Propagation from seed takes too long, so it is preferable to propagate gloriosas from tubers (2). In February or March, plant the tubers in a mix of 1 part leafmould, 1 part loam, 1 part peat and ½ part sand at a pH of 5.5−6.5. Fill largish pots (12−15 cm) (5−6 in) or window-boxes with suitable compost and set the tubers with their buds facing upwards and cover with a 2 cm (¾ in) layer of compost.

The containers should be placed in a room at a temperature of 20−22 °C (68−72 °F). Keep the compost slightly warmer than this and water regularly. Some shade is desirable at the start. Once the tubers have rooted, they can be exposed to full light, as they can bear the sun. The growing shoots should be tied to canes, trellis or nylon netting. Give the plants a weekly dose of compound fertiliser.

After they have flowered in September or October, the leaves will turn yellow and drop. Watering should be stopped altogether at this time and later the dried stems should be removed. The tubers over-winter in dry compost in their containers at a temperature of 5−10 °C (41−50 °F). The new tubers should be carefully detached the following year, then the cultivating cycle is repeated.

The following species are seldom seen in cultivation: the Malabar Lily, *G. superba,* with curled red petals, and *G. simplex* with yellow flowers that gradually turn a reddish yellow.

2

Glory Lilies can be grown in small greenhouses, on verandas and in flower windows. In a favourable climate they can be stood out on balconies and terraces. They grow up to 2 metres (6 ft 6 in) high, opening their flowers in succession during the summer. They are best treated as climbers twining round columns, room dividers and trunks decorated with epiphytic plants. The blooms can also be cut, as they last well in a vase. But the ripe anthers produce a great deal of pollen which can soil the furnishings.

1

131

Guzmania
Guzmania lingulata 'Minor'

Bromeliaceae

Among more than a hundred species of Guzmania growing chiefly in South and Central Amerika, *G. lingulata* 'Minor' is most widely grown as a pot plant. Its narrow, pointed, light green leaves are arranged in a rosette. In the 'Red' cultivar (1) its striking bracts are bright red, whereas the cultivar 'Orange' is a yellowish-orange. The flowers themselves are whitish. Guzmanias average only 25−35 cm (10−14 in) high.

Guzmania is propagated from seed in nurseries. Amateurs do best to propagate them by separating and potting up the daughter plants, which should be done between April and August. Each of the detached plantlets is potted in a 6−7 cm (2½−3 in) pot filled with a mixture of 2 parts coarse leafmould and 1 part peat. An air temperature of 22−25 °C (72−77 °F) with extra heat for the compost and high air humidity are essential to get the plants to root. After several months, guzmanias should be moved into larger pots filled with a mix of 2 parts leafmould, 1 part peat, 1 part pulverised pine bark and ½ part perlite at pH of 4.5−5.5. They need a temperature of 20−22 °C (68−72 °F).

Young plants need regular watering with small doses of water poured into the pot and the leaf rosette. Withhold when winter temperatures fall below 18−20 °C (64−68 °F). Guzmanias do well in diffused light and enjoy partial shade in summer, but when acclimatised, they can stand direct sun or deep shade for a time. Older plants will tolerate dry air in centrally-heated rooms. They should be fed from March to October or November with a solution of compound fertiliser.

3

G. lingulata (2) attains a height of 50 cm (20 in). Their flexible leaves are light green with inconspicuous reddish brown stripes on the underside. The orange-red or red bracts are often yellow or white at the tips, the flowers white.

G. monostachya (3) has a striking tricolor inflorescence which grows well above the leaf rosette. Its bracts are blackish brown at the base, becoming vivid scarlet at the apex of the spike. The flowers are white.

1

2

Guzmanias can be grown on branches
and trunks as epiphytes or set in winter
gardens, flower windows and glass
plant-cases as specimen plants or in
groups.

Haemanthus, Blood Lily
Haemanthus katharinae

Amaryllidaceae

Several dozen species of Haemanthus grow wild in tropical and South Africa. Thanks to their unusual flower heads some of the species became specially interesting to house plant lovers, and are now widely sold.

Haemanthus katharinae (1) has long been one of the most widely cultivated species. Its stem with five or six light green leaves springs from the small bulb together with the flower stem which carries a dense umbel of vermilion-coloured flowers.

The Blood Lily is raised from seed in nurseries, but the only suitable method in our homes is to propagate it from the daughter bulbs in February or March. Pot the bulblets in a mixture of equal parts leafmould and fibrous loam with some sand added at a pH of 5.5−6.5. The bulbs should be placed in a light position and grown on without resting for 1−2 years until they are large enough to flower. The bulbs need regular watering and feeding with a solution of compound fertiliser.

A temperature of 14−18 °C (57−64 °F) is adequate in winter. During the year that flowers are expected, the bulbs should be given tiny amounts of water from October onwards, while they are resting at a temperature of 10−12 °C (50−54 °F), until March. When temperatures rise, the Blood Lily opens its flowers during the summer, if regularly fed and watered.

The bulbs will flower again, so should be repotted in March. Treat them very carefully, so their fragile roots are not damaged.

Crossing *H. katharinae* with *H. puniceus* gave rise to the cultivar 'König Albert' which is more robust than the original

2

Blood Lily, with a more spectacular, blood-red flower head.

The White Paint Brush, *H. albiflos* (2), comes from South Africa. Its short-lived white flowers are borne on a short stout flower stem. The fleshy leaves, thickened at the base, spring directly from the bulb. This plant bears decorative fruits, which ripen even indoors (3). This species overwinters at a temperature of about 10 °C (50 °F) with moderate watering.

Anyone who can provide it with congenial growing conditions can enjoy growing the Blood Lily. But this plant does better in winter gardens and greenhouses than in the home. If cut, the bloom will last quite a long time in a vase.

Common Ivy, English Ivy
Hedera helix

Araliaceae

The original species, *Hedera helix,* is distributed all over Europe. It is a hardy evergreen climber, that reaches a height of 20−30 m (65−98 ft). Ivy finds it difficult to settle in indoor conditions, but in the course of many years of cultivation a great many small-leaved cultivars have arisen, that offer a variety of leaf shapes and colourings. Some of them have become well adapted to the indoor microclimate. The cultivars most frequently offered for sale are 'Glacier', 'Harald', 'Goldheart' (1), 'Pittsburg' (2) and 'Lutzii' (3).

Ivy is easily propagated from tip cuttings all the year round. Several cuttings should be inserted in a 6 cm (2½ in) pot filled with medium-light compost and peat or a mixture of leafmould and soil. They root at a temperature of 16−18 °C (61−64 °F), or lower, preferably in a frame or in a heated greenhouse. Rooted plants should be potted in 10 cm (4 in) pots in the same compost at a pH of 5.5−6.5. Older plants should be repotted between March and June.

Ivies cannot be grown in centrally-heated flats during the winter. The green-leaved cultivars overwinter at 5−10 °C (41−50 °F), some of the variegated forms at 10−18 °C (50−64 °F). Ivy needs a slightly shaded, airy position. Frequent watering is essential during the growing season and even in winter its root ball should never be allowed to dry out. Provide extra air humidity throughout the year by misting. The plants need feeding with a solution of compound fertiliser from March to August.

The Canary Island Ivy, *Hedera canariensis* gave rise to the large-leaved cultivar with white variegation known as 'Gloire de Marengo' (4). This cultivar needs winter

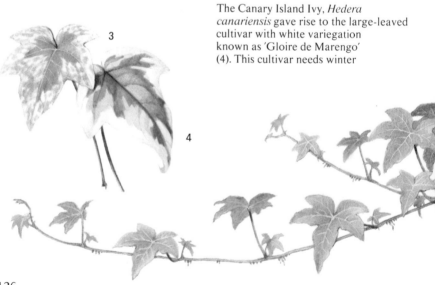

temperatures of 14 – 18 °C (57 – 64 °F), having similar requirements to the cultivars mentioned above.

Too high a temperature, dry air and sometimes gas fumes are the commonest causes of failure with ivies indoors. Ivy plants can be grouped in ceramic bowls with geraniums and some kinds of annuals. Ivies winter well in moderately heated corridors, halls and winter gardens. Some of the hardier cultivars that make more robust growth can be grown on shaded balconies and terraces. In mild winters, ivies can be placed outdoors after hardening off, provided they are well-protected from frost.

2

1

Rose Mallow, Rose of China
Hibiscus rosa-sinensis

Malvaceae

H. rosa-sinensis (1) is grown as an ornamental shrub in the tropical and sub-tropical parts of South East Asia. Cultivars with large single or double flowers, coloured red, pink, yellow or white (2, 3) are cultivated in greenhouses in European nurseries and garden centres. The leaves are long and oval, coarsely toothed and coloured light green.

Rose Mallows are propagated in spring from tip cuttings. Cuttings root in three weeks at a temperature of 22−25 °C (72−77 °F) in high air humidity, preferably in a greenhouse. They root best in small pots covered with plastic sheeting. Rose Mallows grown in the home need a temperature of 18−20 °C (64−68 °F) and a mixture of equal parts leafmould, soil-based compost and peat at a pH of 6.0−6.5. The plants need some shade from the hottest sun, but demand more light while their buds are forming and at flowering time.

Regular watering is essential while they are in active growth, as a shortage of water can cause bud drop. In winter, the temperature should be reduced to 12−15 °C (54−59 °F) and water should be withheld almost entirely. Generous ventilation is advisable at higher temperatures. Rose Mallows are fast growers that demand plenty of feeding, particularly potash, so a solution of compound fertiliser should be given from February to the end of September.

3

Rose Mallows are suitable for seasonal decoration of interiors, particularly in summer. They badly deteriorate and eventually die in overheated rooms where the air is dry in winter.

Bud formation is poor if they have not been given a resting period. Inadequate feeding and over-feeding with nitrogen can have the same effect.

Vigorous, well branched plants are produced by occasional pruning in early spring.

1

2

Amaryllis, Hippeastrum
Hippeastrum hybrids

Amaryllidaceae

Several dozen species of Hippeastrum grow wild in Central and South America. But nowadays, only specially bred hybrids are found in cultivation (1). They vary in the colour and size of their flowers, in the number of flowers per stem and in their flowering time. The flowers are various shades of red, pink and white, some of them striped in two colours. Hippeastrum is propagated from daughter bulbs or from seed. Both methods demand a lot of the gardener's time, as they have to be carried out in a greenhouse. However, if a flowering plant has produced some daughter bulbs, which does not commonly happen, they can be grown on separately to develop into flowering bulbs.

To grow a hippeastrum well it is best to start with a purchased bulb in autumn. After flowering, cut back the remains of the flower and its stem close to the top of the bulb. Stand the bulb in a light position, eventually out in the garden, after the end of May. Liberal watering and a temperature of 18−25 °C (64−77 °F) are essential. Weekly doses of nitrogenous fertiliser should be given, then replaced by a fertiliser high in phosphate in July. Increase the air humidity by spraying the foliage frequently. During the hot summer months, the plants should be slightly shaded to protect their foliage from sunscorch.

From August onwards, feeding should be stopped and watering gradually reduced, then withheld. Plants standing outside should be protected from rain as the resting period sets in. This is vitally important for the formation of next year's flowers. Before winter arrives, the plants should be moved into a room at a temperature of 10−12 °C (50−54 °F).

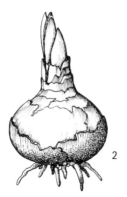

2

In January, the dried leaves should be removed and the bulbs (2) moved into larger pots filled with a mixture of peat and pure, medium heavy topsoil or fibrous loam, at a pH of 6.0−7.0. A 20 g (3/4 oz) dose of powdered compound fertiliser should be added to every litre of compost and the temperature should be increased to 15−17 °C (59−63 °F). The newly potted bulbs should be watered only once. Regular watering should then

140

1

be continued when the flower stem has elongated. The temperature should be increased to 20–22 °C (68–72 °F) by this time and kept up until the buds begin to colour. The life of the flowers can be lengthened by dropping the temperature to 14–16 °C (57–61 °F). Poor flowering of hippeastrums is for the most part caused by too short a rest period, or none at all, or inadequate feeding of the bulbs during the summer.

141

Howea, Curly Palm, Sentry Palm
Howea belmoreana
syn. *Kentia belmoreana*

Palmae

The Howea genus was originally confined to the Pacific Island. *Howea belmoreana* (1) is the species most widely found in greenhouse gardens and used by floral decorators. In indoor conditions Howea can reach a height of 3 metres (10 ft) or even more. Its simple, narrow leaves with reddish petioles arch over. The lower part of the stem is largely devoid of foliage, so Howeas are usually grouped together with lower-growing plants in large containers or grown three together in a large pot.

They are propagated from imported seeds (2). In winter, Howea is grown in a room temperature of 16—22 °C (61—72 °F), though older plants will tolerate 12—16 °C (54—61 °F). Direct sunlight can damage the young leaves, so the plant is best placed in diffused light or in semi-shade. Though Howea can manage without much light, its growth becomes stunted when it is grown in deep shade.

Where it is kept in a warm room in winter, the compost should be kept just moist, but in general, the water supply should be cut back from November to mid-February. It should be watered freely and sprayed frequently during its active growing season. Repotting is necessary every two years between March and August. The most suitable growing medium is a porous, nutritious soil-based compost, such as a mix of 1 part John Innes compost with the addition of 1 part peat at a pH of 5.0—6.5. Howea should be fed from March to October, with a solution of compound fertiliser high in nitrogen.

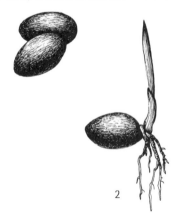

The Paradise Palm, *Howea forsteriana,* has many features in common with the previous species, though older plants are more slender and carry their green-stemmed leaves in a looser arrangement.

Howeas are suitable for decorating spacious, airy interiors, like large winter gardens, entrance halls and palm houses. Mature plants flower from April to August and later bear yellowish-green fruits.

The Chinese Fan Palm, *Livistona chinensis,* can be grown similarly. Its fan-like leaves are split halfway to the centre into separate segments. This species demands more light and cannot be compared to the howeas for durability. After many years these palms can reach a height of 150 cm (5 ft) indoors.

2

1

Hoya, Wax Plant
Hoya carnosa

Asclepiadaceae

The various kinds of Hoya originated in the tropics of East Asia and Australia. Of these *H. carnosa* (1) makes the best house plant. It climbs or trails and its shoots are best trained up supports. The fleshy evergreen leaves measure 5—8 cm (2—3 in) long and 3—4 cm (1 1/4—1 1/2 in) across. Its large fragrant white or pink flowers are borne in dense umbels.

The Wax Plant is propagated from cuttings with one pair of leaves and root best at a temperature of 20—25 °C (68—77 °F). Cuttings are inserted in an equal parts mix of peat and sand and covered with plastic. From three to five rooted cuttings are inserted in a 10—12 cm (4—5 in) pot filled with a porous mixture of 2 parts loam, 1 part peat and 1/2 part sand at a pH of 5.5—6.5. Hoya likes a summer temperature of 18—22 °C (64—72 °F), but in winter, a light position at a temperature of 12—15 °C (54—59 °F) is sufficient.

Young plants need shading slightly but adult plants will stand full light. From spring to autumn, water regularly, but from November onwards plants should be watered just enough to keep the compost from drying out. Make sure they are given adequate fresh air, preferably not too dry.

Hoya should be repotted every year between May and August. A solution of compound fertiliser should be given from April to August.

2

Do not cut back the flowered shoots, as they bear umbels of flowers on sideshoots the following year. The plants should not be moved after their buds have begun to colour.

Hoya carnosa tends to live a long time in flats and other kinds of interiors. It can be stood on its own on shelves or windowsills or displayed near a latticed room divider. The Wax Plant grows very well in a soilless medium.

144

The less widely grown *Hoya bella* (2) has a more delicate habit, smaller leaves, and its umbels of flowers are less dense. This species requires a warmer, more humid environment than *H. carnosa*.

Hoya longifolia has rather delicate shoots and leathery leaves. Its flowers are similar to those of *H. bella*.

1

Hydrangea
Hydrangea macrophylla

Hydrangeaceae

Several dozen shrubby, tree-like and climbing species of hydrangea grow wild in North and South America, China and Japan, as well as on the Philippine Islands and Java. *H. macrophylla* (1), a native of Japan, is of prime importance in horticulture. This species has given rise to a range of cultivars varying in colour, flower size, flowering time and habit of growth.

It is difficult to raise a flowering hydrangea plant from a cutting in indoor conditions, so the indoor plant enthusiast should focus his efforts on caring well for plants bought already in flower. Hydrangeas should be placed in a light position in a temperature of 14−18 °C (57−64 °F). They should be watered liberally, so the water soaks the soil ball and fills a dish placed under the pot. They like the air as humid as possible. Do not expose flowering plants to direct sunlight.

After flowering the flower head should be cut back, the shoots pruned and the plant repotted in a mix of 1 part loam, 2 parts peat and 1 part sand at a pH of 4.5−5.5. The pots should be plunged in an unshaded garden bed. Weekly doses of compound fertiliser high in nitrogen should be given from May onwards, but a fertiliser with a normal balance of nutrients is most suitable in July and August.

From September onwards watering should be restricted and feeding becomes unnecessary. Before the frosts arrive, hydrangeas should be moved into a light, cool, well-ventilated room and kept unwatered at a temperature of 5−8 °C (41−46 °F) until the beginning of January, when they can be moved into a room at a temperature of 16−18 °C (61−64 °F). Here, hydrangeas will flower again, provided they are given high air humidity, watered regularly and fed twice a week.

2

Hydrangeas bear white, pink or red flowers. Blue-coloured bracts are produced by adding 5 g (1/5 oz) of alum to 1 litre of compost.

Hydrangea paniculata (2), which bears white flowers which age to pink, reaches a height of 3.6 m (12 ft). It is grown out in the garden throughout the year, with its roots and bottom branches protected from hard frost.

1

Hydrangeas last well in the home at
low temperatures. They are suitable for
decorating graves, and are also bedded
out or grouped in ceramic bowls.

147

Bay Laurel, Sweet Bay
Laurus nobilis

Lauraceae

Laurus nobilis (1) is one of the most typical woody plants (2) of the Mediterranean area. Cultivated forms of this evergreen tree or shrub grow up to 150—200 cm (5—6½ ft) tall. The leaves are thin, glossy, lanceolate with slightly curled margins. The inconspicuous yellowish flowers open in April and May.

The Sweet Bay is propagated from tip cuttings between September and April. Cuttings root in equal parts of sand and peat at a temperature of 16—20 °C (61—68 °F). The rooted cuttings are then potted in a nutritious compost formed of 1 part peat and 2 parts loam with ½ part of sand at a pH of 6.0—7.5.

Young plants should be moved into larger pots each year between February and April. Older plants can be repotted every 2—4 years. If planted in too large a container, Sweet Bays root poorly and the surplus soil turns acid, eventually killing them. When repotting, add 2—4 g (0.07—0.14 oz) of compound fertiliser to each litre of soil. While the plants are in active growth, give fortnightly doses of a compound fertiliser high in nitrogen.

Sweet Bays overwinter happily in a light room at a temperature of 2—5 °C (36—41 °F). They should be generously ventilated at temperatures above 8 °C (46 °F). The previous year's shoots should be pruned in early spring. In late May, the plants can be placed out in the garden, in arbours and on balconies and terraces. Laurels don't need shading. Watering should be ample and regular in summer. It helps to spray the foliage with water on hot days, but the compost should not be kept permanently wet.

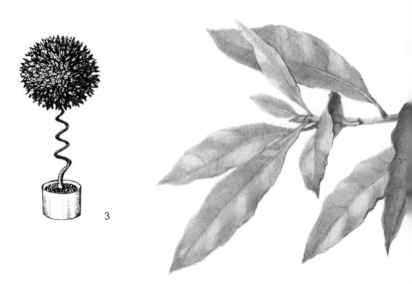

3

Mature Sweet Bays are among the loveliest of ornamental woody plants. They are most widely grown as pyramids or ball-shaped specimens (3).

It takes 8—10 years to raise a large plant, obviously too long for a home gardener to raise one in the home. So it is recommended to buy a good-sized specimen, whose price will naturally be in scale with the length of time it has been growing. Thanks to its favourable climate, Belgium is the world's largest producer of Sweet Bays.

2

1

Maranta, Prayer Plant
Maranta leuconeura

Marantaceae

Some 20 species of Maranta grow wild in the humid tropical forests of South America. *M. leuconeura* and some of its cultivars are of major importance as ornamental plants. Maranta is an evergreen perennial plant growing up to 25—30 cm (10—12 in) tall. Its wide elliptical leaves are emerald green on the upper side, with regularly arranged white and dark green markings on each side of the midrib. The underside is a purplish green.

The Prayer Plant is propagated between February and May from cuttings, or by dividing good-sized plants. Cuttings are quick to root in an air temperature of 20—22 °C (68—72 °F) with the compost temperature 2 °C (4 °F) higher. They root best when placed under a polythene covering or in a greenhouse. High air humidity is essential not only while they are rooting, but throughout their lives.

Mature plants are grown at a winter temperature of 18—22 °C (64—72 °F) in semi-shade as they cannot stand direct sun. Marantas have a high water consumption, so they require regular and ample watering throughout the summer. Cut down the supply of water from November to February, in step with the fall in temperature. Frequent misting is desirable.

Repotting is best done from February to May in a mixture of 2 parts leafmould, 1 part loam and 1 part peat at a pH of 5.0—6.5. Marantas grow quite rapidly, so they need regular feeding with a compound fertiliser. Give them the fertiliser once a week from February to October, but none in the winter.

2

The cultivar *M. leuconeura* 'Kerchoveana' (2) is now widely grown in nurseries. It is notable for its more spectacular colouring, but needs the same conditions as the original species.

M. leuconeura 'Erythroneura' (1) has a more robust appearance than the other two plants.

In centrally-heated homes, marantas can only be grown successfully in shaded flower windows and tropical cases, planted singly or in twos and threes. Marantas are occasionally planted in ceramic bowls with some flowering plants that have a short season of beauty.

1

Monstera, Swiss Cheese Plant
Monstera deliciosa

Araceae

Monstera deliciosa (1), which originated in the South American tropics, is notable for its large leathery dark green lobed leaves. The leaves of older plants are generously perforated. This plant is a climber, growing several metres long in indoor conditions. Its rather woody stem puts out long greenish brown aerial roots. Mature plants flower from May to October. The spathe is creamy white and the spadix is greenish in colour (2).

Monstera demands no special growing conditions. It does best at temperatures of 18−22 °C (64−72 °F), but older plants tolerate winter temperatures ranging from 12−15 °C (54−59 °F). They are best grown in semi-shade, as their leaves turn yellow when exposed to full sun. Though monsteras will survive if placed some distance from the light, they then have smaller leaves without any lobes or perforations. They thrive in a peaty compost or in a mixture of equal parts peat and leafmould. The pH reaction should be adjusted to 5.5−6.5.

While young, the plants should be repotted every year but older ones need this attention only every 2−3 years between March and August. Water them liberally. These plants do well in centrally-heated homes where the air is dry. Monsteras should be fed with fortnightly doses of a compound fertiliser high in nitrogen. Stop feeding from October to February.

They are propagated from tip cuttings inserted in 12−14 cm (4½−5½ in) pots filled with peat containing no fertiliser.

2

The cultivar *M. deliciosa* 'Borsigiana' has smaller ornamental leaves.

Monsteras are long-lived plants. Do not cut back the aerial roots, as they help to feed the plant if inserted in the compost. The gardener can take advantage of this, particularly with large plants. All monsteras thrive in hydroponic solutions. They are suitable for decorating large spaces of all kinds.

1

Myrtle
Myrtus communis

Myrtaceae

About a hundred species of Myrtus grow in the sub-tropical parts of America and Australia. The popular *M. communis* (1) is a native of the Mediterranean countries, and grows into a shrub up to 5 m (16½ ft) high in its natural habitat. The myrtle has small entire, lanceolate leathery leaves, fragrant when rubbed. The fragrant white flowers bear masses of yellow stamens (2). The fruits (3) are reddish and later turn bluish black.

Propagation is by means of tip or stem cuttings, which root best when inserted in peat and sand and grown in slight shade at a temperature of 14−18 °C (57−64 °F). Rooting is hastened by covering them with a sheet of glass or plastic. Young plants are grown in a light compost at a temperature of 18−20 °C (64−68 °F). A temperature of about 4−6 °C (39−43 °F) is best for bringing the plants through the winter. Older plants should be repotted between February and May in a mix of 1 part loam, 1 part leafmould and ½ part sand at a pH of 5.0−6.0. Hardened plants can be grown without shade, for in their native lands myrtles grow in full sun.

Correct watering is vital. The root balls should never dry out, but an excess of water will cause yellowing foliage. Water cautiously while temperatures are low in winter. Feed throughout the growing season, from February to September, with a solution of compound fertiliser. At the start, extra nitrogen is desirable, but in August and September the plants should be given feeds with a higher potash content. Do not feed at all while they are flowering. The plants should not be pruned at this time either and watering should be limited.

3

When spring frosts are over, myrtles can be grown out in the garden on balconies or terraces or on windowsills. This shrub stands up well to shaping. Trim young plants to develop better branching. Older plants can be shaped into pyramids or low-growing trees with a spherical head. The more often the protruding shoots are pruned all along the tree top, the more compact growth is created, though flowering is discouraged somewhat.

Myrtle is one of the oldest cultivated
plants. It has been written about ever
since ancient times, and forms
a traditional part of wedding decorations.

155

Neoregelia
Neoregelia carolinae 'Tricolor'

Bromeliaceae

Neoregelia carolinae is an epiphyte native to eastern Brazil. In its cultivar 'Tricolor' (1), the leathery leaves form a compact rosette. They are about 30 cm (12 in) long and green with yellowish white longitudinal stripes. In young plants, the centre of the rosette is inconspicuous in colour, but when mature the leaf bases and bracts turn bright red before flowering begins. The small bluish violet flowers open in succesion deep in the centre of the rosette.

Neoregelia is propagated in the home from the offsets that form beside the main rosette, when their leaves have grown 12−15 cm (4¾−6 in) long. Any time from February to September, they should be inserted in 6−7 cm (2½−2¾ in) pots filled with a mixture of 1 part coarse leafmould, 2 parts peat and 1 part shredded bark with some perlite added, at a pH of 4.5−5.5. A temperature of 22−25 °C (72−77 °F) is desirable throughout this period. Older plants do well at an air and soil temperature of 20−22 °C (68−72 °F).

Soft water, preferably tepid, should be poured into the leaf rosette regularly during the summer. Keep the compost slightly moist throughout the year, but the centre of the rosette should be dry during the winter. Mist over the foliage on hot days. Plants do well in partial shade. Insufficient light results in poor colouring of the bracts. Feed the plants from February to November, preferably with a weak solution of compound fertiliser.

2

3

Several species of Nidularium often mistaken for neoregelias, have similar growing requirements. *N. fulgens* (2), *N. procerum* and *N. innocentii* (3) are the

1

most widely cultivated. All have red
bracts arranged in a compact rosette.

Neoregelias and nidulariums can be
grown in large flower windows and
tropical cases. They can also be displayed
on large trunks with other epiphytes.
Mature plants thrive in dry conditions in
centrally-heated homes.

Sword Fern, Boston Fern
Nephrolepis exaltata

Polypodiaceae

The species *N. exaltata* (1), distributed in the tropics of all parts of the world, gave rise to a number of cultivars, which are among the most widely cultivated ferns. They are notable for their long pinnate fronds with wavy leaflets of various shapes. The cultivars 'Bostoniensis Nana' (2), 'Rooseveltii Plumosa', 'Maassii', 'Hillii', 'Teddy Junior' (3) and others are now grown as pot plants.

Sword ferns are propagated from the young plants produced on their spreading runners. The plantlets should be potted in 5—6 cm (2—2½ in) pots filled with fibrous peat (pH ± 5.0), slightly shaded and sheltered with a sheet of plastic or glass. Provide them with a temperature of 20—22 °C (68—72 °F) and maximum air humidity. Older plants will tolerate a temperature of 15—18 °C (59—64 °F) during the winter. They need a light, fairly humid position, but cannot stand direct sunlight.

The best time of repotting is between April and June. The most suitable compost is an equal parts mixture of peat and loam with a pH of 5.0—6.0. During the summer, sword ferns need regular watering with soft water, left to stand overnight, and frequent misting. When temperatures are lower in winter, watering should be reduced and done only in the morning so the fronds do not stay wet overnight. The cultivars do not generally thrive in centrally-heated rooms.

Sword ferns should be fed every 10 days from April to August with a solution of compound fertiliser.

The Sword Fern can also be grown in a soilless medium. Provided its surroundings are not excessively warm, this fern should last a considerable time. Potted plants are suitable for decorating winter gardens, halls and large flower windows.

The Fishtail or Holly Fern, *Cyrtomium falcatum* (syn. *Polystichum falcatum*) is less widely grown, despite being quite long-lived in moderately heated rooms and winter gardens. Its pinnate fronds are coarse and glossy. This fern overwinters at a temperature of 8—15 °C (46—59 °F).

The delicate *Phlebodium aureum* 'Glaucum', where fronds are a bluish grey colour, ranks among the most valued plants. It can also be grown as an epiphyte.

2

3

1

159

Oleander
Nerium oleander

Apocynaceae

Nerium oleander (1) is among the most widely distributed shrubs around the Mediterranean. It has narrow leathery leaves and in natural conditions reaches a height of 3—6 m (10—20 ft). Its pink or yellow flowers are borne in irregular terminal clusters and are pleasantly scented. In our different climatic conditions, the cultivated hybrids start flowering in June, with red, pink (2), white or yellow blooms, and continue flowering until October.

The oleander is propagated from tip cuttings between February and August. They root in a mixture of peat and sand or in clear water, at a temperature of 16—20 °C (61—68 °F) preferably in slight shade. A temperature of 2—6 °C (36—43 °F) and a light, well-ventilated position is adequate for overwintering mature plants. Between March and May, plants should be repotted in a mixture of equal parts loam, peat and sand at a pH of 6.0—7.5. Long roots can be trimmed when repotting.

Liberal watering with tepid water is necessary from spring to autumn. A layer of drainage material (gravel or crushed brick) should be put in the bottom of the pot to stop excess water rotting the roots. Water sparingly during the winter. Regular weekly feeds should be given, using a solution of compound fertiliser.

Oleanders need a sunny, warm, though airy position in summer.

Oleanders are rewarding ornamentals. During the summer they can be grown successfully out on balconies and terraces or in arbours. Light unheated halls, corridors and stair-cases are suitable for them in winter.

The Bottlebrush, *Callistemon citrinus,* can be grown similarly. This hardy,

2

160

evergreen woody species is native to
Australia. Its branches end in the typical
red inflorescences reminiscent of
a bottlebrush. But you will rarely find this
plant for sale. It is used in the same ways
as the oleander. The Bottlebrush needs
slight shade on very hot, sunny days.

1

Pachystachys, Lollipop Plant
Pachystachys lutea

Acanthaceae

Pachystachys lutea (1) comes from the tropics of Central and South America, where it forms a shrub several metres high. It is remarkable for its spiky flower heads with rich yellow bracts, which last for a long time in the home. The attractiveness of this plant is often marred by the loss of the leaves from its bottom branches, usually caused by too dry an atmosphere.

This plant should be grown in a light spot, at a winter temperature of 20−22 °C (68−72 °F). It benefits from slight shading in summer. Water the plants cautiously throughout the winter, as a waterlogged root ball will cause yellowing foliage. The compost should be kept moist all the time and the aerial parts of the plant misted frequently during the growing season.

The plants are best repotted between February and May in a mixture of 2 parts leafmould, 1 part peat and 1 part sand at a pH 5.5−6.0. The branches should be pruned hard at this time, to get good branching and compact growth. Propagation is from tip or stem cuttings, preferably young shoots from cut-back plants. Cuttings root in compost with some bottom heat and an air temperature of 22−25 °C (72−77 °F). They root best in a mixture of peat and sand. Rooted cuttings can be potted three to a pot.

A solution of compound fertiliser should be given from March to August. This plant needs extra potash at the end of its growing period.

2

The less widely grown *P. coccinea* (2) displays a pinkish red inflorescence of different shape.

Pachystachys is not suitable for growing in centrally-heated homes, though it makes a lovely room decoration while in flower. Plants grown in flower windows, glass plant-cases and well-heated winter gardens with high air humidity will last much longer in good condition.

Pachystachys is often mistaken for the Shrimp Plant, *Beloperone guttata* (3). This plant has similar cultivation requirements, but bears a rather different, drooping inflorescence, usually with many more flowers. The pendulous forms are usually grown in hanging bowls.

Pandanus, Screw Pine
Pandanus veitchii

Pandanaceae

Screw pines are among the largest plants grown indoors. They came originally from the tropics of Africa, Asia and Australia. In indoor conditions, *P. veitchii* (1) can grow up to 2 m (6 ft 6 in) high and about the same across. Its long sessile, sword-like leaves grow spirally on the short stem and are a deep green with white-striped margins. Screw pines form strong prop roots raising the neck of the plant above soil level.

These plants grow well at a temperature of 20−22 °C (68−72 °F). Winter temperatures that fall below 15 °C (59 °F) for any length of time can damage their foliage and roots. The plants should be grown in slight shade throughout the summer. Screw pines will survive some distance from à window, but they have a much poorer leaf colour in these conditions. They dislike direct sunshine, however. Screw pines are best grown in a mixture of equal parts peat and loam at a pH of 5.5−6.5. They should be repotted each year into a pot 2−4 cm (¾−1½ in) larger than the previous one.

Water liberally throughout the year, withholding it only if there is a severe drop in temperature. Keep as high air humidity as possible to prevent the leaf tips drying out. Feed at regular weekly intervals with a solution of compound fertiliser, except during the winter.

Screw pines are propagated by separating and potting up the shoots that spring up at the base of the stems of older plants.

2

P. baptistii (2) has narrower, smooth fluted leaves with yellow stripes.
P. pacificus (3) makes lower growth. Its short pointed dark green leaves are broader than in screw pines, at some 10−12 cm (4−4¾ in) across. This species sometimes suffers from chlorosis of the leaves.

As these plants demand so much space, they have only a limited range of uses. They are suitable for decorating light, spacious rooms, such as halls and glazed porches. Pandanuses are long-lived provided they are grown in favourable growing conditions.

1

3

Paphiopedilum, Slipper Orchid, Lady's Slipper

Orchidaceae

Paphiopedilum hybrids

Though many orchid genera, species and cultivars are found in cultivation, none has adapted itself to the average microclimatic conditions so well that it could be called a true house plant. Air-conditioned tropical cases, closed flower windows and winter gardens remain the only possible places for growing orchids successfully.

From the horticultural point of view, the hybrid *P.* × *maudiae* (1) is among the most highly valued of orchids, chiefly because it has no fixed flowering season. During the winter, this hybrid does best in partial shade at a temperature of 16−20 °C (61−68 °F). The same applies to other species of Paphiopedilum, apart from *P. insigne.*

Slipper orchids are propagated by division, preferably between February and June. The compost should be of a coarse texture. A mixture of fibrous peat, crushed pine bark and perlite is generally most suitable. The pH should range from 5.0−6.0.

Slipper orchids should be well watered from March to November, but the supply should be cut back during the winter, at lower temperatures and while growth is limited. Keep up high air humidity throughout the year. Feed with great care at fortnightly intervals from March to October, with a weak solution of compound fertiliser.

3

Apart from the large-flowered Paphiopedilum hybrids, several species are suitable for cultivation, such as the cool-growing *P. insigne,* as well as *P. lawrenceanum, P. harrisianum, P. callosum* and *P. rothschildianum.* As the demands of the various species differ somewhat, it is only wise to start growing orchids after acquiring considerable theoretical knowledge about them.

Among other valued orchids that can be grown in the conditions described are the *Cattleya* hybrids (2), as well as those belonging to the *Vanda, Dendrobium* and *Oncidium* genera.

Species like *Phalaenopsis luedde-manniana* (3) as well as the Phalaenopsis hybrids flower almost throughout the year, given a winter temperature of 21−23 °C (70−73 °F).

Passiflora, Passion Flower
Passiflora caerulea

Passifloraceae

The Passifloras number more than 400 woody and herbaceous climbers growing wild in the tropics and sub-tropics right round the world. A native of the South American tropical forests, *P. caerulea* (1), bears blue flowers from spring to autumn. The Passion Flower used to be widely grown on internal windowsills, but it has now lost much of its value as a pot plant, mainly because it needs a temperature of only 10—12 °C (50—54 °F) during its winter rest period. As such conditions are not found in modern homes, the Passion Flower is hardly seen in cultivation nowadays.

The Passion Flower is propagated from stem cuttings with three leaves between March and June. The cuttings root within three weeks, preferably in peat and sand at a temperature of 18—22 °C (64—72 °F). They should be covered with a sheet of glass or plastic. When rooted, Passion Flowers should be potted in a heavier mixture, usually consisting of good loam, peat and sand at pH 6.0—7.5. If planted in a light mixture, the plant does not flower well. Conditions are most favourable for repotting from March to May. Older plants should be pruned annually in early spring, the shoots being cut back to leave only four or five leaf buds.

Water the plants freely during the summer, as the plentiful foliage transpires a lot of water. In low winter temperatures, on the other hand, the water supply should be cut back.

The plants need a light position throughout the year, except while being propagated and for a time after repotting, when partial shade is desirable. Plants standing in deep shade do not flower well.

2

In the home, passion flowers can only be grown in moderately heated rooms. They do better in winter gardens where the temperature is controlled and in conservatories, where they grow several metres high, bearing handsome flowers in summer. Potted plants are trained up wooden or metal supports. Some of the large-flowered cultivars, bearing white, pink or violet flowers, are more highly valued than the species itself.

The Red Cluster Passion Flower,

P. racemosa, has larger leaves and
crimson-red flowers, which appear in late
summer and during the autumn.
    The Granadilla, P. edulis (2), is
distinguished from P. caerulea by the
striking wavy filaments of its corolla.

1

Ivy-leaved Geranium
Pelargonium peltatum hybrids

Geraniaceae

Hybrids of *Pelargonium peltatum* (1, 2) are very popular with indoor gardeners. Their pendulous shoots are smooth and hairless and their glossy leaves of a similar shape to the ivy's. Besides the typical ivy-leaved geranium cultivars, others derived from the crossing of *P. zonale* and *P. peltatum* can also be found in cultivation. They bear similar shaped leaves to *P. peltatum,* but their growth is upright. Both kinds are suitable for growing in window and balcony boxes as well as in hanging baskets.

Geraniums are propagated from tip cuttings by August at the latest as plants propagated later cannot reach a sufficient size by the following May. Insert at least three cuttings in a pot filled with peat and sand. During the winter, geraniums should be grown in a light position at a temperature of 8−12 °C (46−54 °F). In March they should be planted out in tubs or windowboxes under cover filled with a mix of equal parts peat and loam at a pH of 6.0−6.5. Water them cautiously. The shoots should be pinched back two or three times to get good branching.

In late May after hardening off, flowering geraniums planted in flower boxes can be placed outside, where they will flower in full sun till the autumn. A solution of compound fertiliser should be given at fortnightly intervals from May to August.

The other popular two groups of geranium are the hybrids of *P. zonale,* the Zonal Geranium, and *P.* × *domesticum* or Regal Pelargonium.

Hybrids of *P. zonale* (3) are grown in windowboxes. Low-growing varieties can be planted in garden bowls or flower beds. They are propagated from tip cuttings in July, or in January. Cuttings should be left to wilt a little before they are inserted in compost to reduce the risk of rotting. Each cutting should be potted in a separate pot once it has rooted.

Hybrids of *P.* × *domesticum* (4) differ from the preceding plants in the growing

conditions they need and in their range of uses. The long-established varieties bloom from April to July. They can be displayed in bowls and windowboxes, and grow well in cool rooms as well. Low-growing repeat-flowering varieties flower throughout the summer. Large-flowered geraniums are more sensitive to fierce sunshine as well as to continuous rainy weather, which causes poor flowering.

Peperomia, Pepper Elder
Peperomia obtusifolia 'Variegata'

Piperaceae

Most of the different kinds of Peperomia we grow as indoor plants originated in the tropics of South and Central America, where they grow in humid forests in a thick layer of moss and humus. They generally have a low habit of growth, bearing stiff or soft leaves of different colours. *P. obtusifolia* 'Variegata' (1) has upright stems with glossy leaves variegated yellowish white. It is propagated between the end of February and September from stem cuttings, which should be planted three to five to a pot of small bowl. They root at a temperature of 20—24 °C (68—75 °F) in slight shade, preferably in a mixture of peat and sand.

During the winter, mature plants should be grown at a temperature of 16—18 °C (61—64 °F) in high air humidity. In summer, plants do well in a sunny spot. A spell of morning sun is good for developing proper leaf colouring, but long exposure to hot sun, particularly if accompanied by low air humidity, causes the leaves to deteriorate.

From March to September, watering should be generous and the gardener should make sure the air humidity is as high as possible. But overwatering in winter can set up root rot. Peperomias should be repotted from February to September when the plant has rooted through the pot. A mix of 2 parts peat and 1 part loam forms a suitable compost. Adjust the pH to 5.0—6.5. Feed with a compound fertiliser solution fortnightly from April to September.

Peperomias with an upright habit include a vast group of species with short stems and leaves springing up a soil level. This group includes the species *P. caperata* (2) with ornamental flower spikes, and the Watermelon Peperomia or Rugby Football Plant, *P. argyreia,* bearing silver-striped leaves. Both species are propagated from leaf cuttings.

P. serpens and the Wax Privet, *Peperomia glabella,* have a pendulous habit of growth. As a general rule the soft-leaved species and cultivars need a higher winter temperature of about 18—20 °C (64—68 °F), while the

1

soft-leaved ones will stand a temporary
fall in winter temperatures to 15 °C
(59 °F). Peperomias rarely grow
successfully in centrally-heated homes
but those planted out in open soil in
tropical cases and warm, humid flower
windows will thrive for a long time.

Philodendron, Parlour Ivy

Araceae

Philodendron scandens

Philodendrons occur widely in the tropical parts of Central and South America, where they grow as terrestrial or semi-epiphytic lianas, trees and shrubs. *P. scandens* (1) is one of the longest-lived species among the diverse range of philodendrons in cultivation. It is a climbing or pendulous plant with glossy dark green leaves borne on its slender stem. It can be propagated from stem cuttings almost all the year round. Insert from five to seven cuttings in a 7−9 cm (3−3½ in) pot. They root well in a mixture of 1 part peat and ½ part sand at a temperature of 22−26 °C (72−79 °F). The philodendron can be grown at winter temperatures of about 15−22 °C (59−72 °F) as it is not fussy about fluctuating temperatures. This plant does well in a slightly shaded position, but also tolerates deep shade. From February to November water regularly to keep the compost permanently moist. In December and January water should be given sparingly. Young plants need high air humidity but mature ones adapt very well to indoor conditions.

Plants should be repotted between March and August in a mixture of 2 parts leafmould, 1 part loam and 1 part peat at a pH of 5.5−6.5. They benefit from regular feeding from March to October with a solution of compound fertiliser. *P. scandens* can reach a length of 3−4 metres (10−13 ft).

3

2

The Fiddle Leaf or Horse's Head,
P. pandureiforme (2), is one of the
philodendrons with medium-sized leaves,
which do well in indoor conditions.
It grows more slowly than *P. scandens.*
It is often secured to canes covered with
sphagnum moss, to which its aerial roots
can cling.

The Blushing Philodendron, *P. imbe* (3),
bears large, oblong sagittate leaves,
reddish on the underside. The petioles
and stem are coloured with typical
reddish spots. This is a climber suitable
for decorating spacious rooms and
glassed-in halls.

1

175

Phoenix, Canary Island Palm
Phoenix canariensis

Palmae

Eleven species of Phoenix grow in tropical Africa and Asia. *P. canariensis* (1), a native of the Canary Islands, adapts very well to indoor conditions. It can be grown in rooms at a temperature of 14—18 °C (57—64 °F), but the higher the winter temperature, the higher the air humidity should be. Older plants overwinter at a temperature of about 10 °C (50 °F). They should be placed in a light position, preferably close to a window. During the summer, large phoenix palms can be placed outside after hardening off and grown in full sun.

Phoenix palms are propagated from imported seeds (2) sown straight in small pots filled with equal parts of peat and sand. The pots should be placed in a propagator. Good-sized plants should be repotted every two years between March and August in a medium-heavy soil mixture, such as 2 or 3 parts good loam to 1 part peat at a pH of 5.0—6.5. Or of course in a proprietary soil-based potting compost such as John Innes. Cover the bottom of the pot with a layer of drainage material about 4—10 cm (1½—4 in) deep.

Feeding should continue from February to November, using a solution of compound fertiliser. Older plants demand quite a lot of feeding.

Ample watering is desirable from spring to autumn, but from November to January cut back the water supply in line with the room temperature. Keep the air humidity as high as possible.

2

P. reclinata bears much-divided arching fronds. It needs a slightly shaded position, but if the light is too poor the inadequately developed petioles make the leaves curve abnormally. Permanent shortage of light can even cause the leaves to crack. The optimum winter temperature is about 16—20 °C (61—68 °F), though this plant can come through the winter at only 8—10 °C (46—50 °F).

Young phoenix palms make very decorative indoor plants, while mature ones are suitable for decorating spacious halls, winter gardens and club rooms.

1

Before a plant is moved out on to
a terrace or into the garden, the room
should be generously ventilated and the
foliage gradually exposed to direct
sunlight.

177

Pilea, Aluminium Plant
Pilea cadierei

More than 200 species of Pilea are distributed in the tropical forests of America and Asia. These mat-forming perennial plants grow in deep shade. *P. cadierei* (1) is the best for decorative purposes. Its opposite leaves are oblong to oval with a conspicuous silvery grey variegation. This plant forms underground suckers and is quick to branch, growing up to 40 cm (15½ in) tall.

This Pilea is easily propagated from tip cuttings which root quickly in a light sandy soil at a temperature of 16–18 °C (61–64 °F), preferably between January and August. During the winter, the plant should be grown about 1–2 m (3 ft 3 in–6 ft 6 in) from a window. In summer it can be moved into deep shade and grown at a temperature of 16–20 °C (61–68 °F). Water freely from February to September but sparsely at other times. Keep the air humidity as high as possible, for dry air as well as direct sun can damage the leaves and cause them to drop.

Repotting is best done from March to April in a medium light compost with sand added, at a pH of 5.5–6.5. The container should not be too large, so the plant does not become waterlogged.

Compound fertilisers with a balanced ratio of major nutrients are best for feeding from April to August. *Pilea cadierei* can also be grown hydroponically.

2

The Artillery Plant, *Pilea microphylla*, (*P. muscosa*) is a mat-forming species suitable for growing in warm or cool winter gardens, flower windows and greenhouses. Its tiny soft leaves are borne on stout fleshy shoots. In summer this plant can be grown with annuals in shaded flower beds.

The Panamiga or Friendship Plant,

1

Pilea spruceana (2), like the preceding
species, comes from South America. Its
wrinkled leaves are a brownish-green
colour. This plant has a low creeping
habit with greenish-white flowers at the
ends of its stems. It can be grown in small
bowls stood in semi-shade. It can also
form the underplanting in winter gardens
and flower windows.

Platycerium, Stag's Horn Fern
Platycerium bifurcatum

Polypodiaceae

Platyceriums are epiphytic ferns that grow in the tropics of Asia, Africa and Australia. They bear two distinct types of foliage of different shape — the barren fronds or mantle leaves and the fertile fronds. The simple broad barren fronds are borne at the base of the plant. They often help the plant to get attached to the bark, sheltering the roots at the same time but gradually die off. The fertile fronds are about 40−80 cm (15¾−31½ in) long, curved over and forked. They have both photosynthetic and reproductive functions. *P. bifurcatum* (1) grows about 1 metre (3 ft 3 in) high in greenhouse conditions. Older plants bear brown sporangia (2) on the undersides of the fertile fronds.

The Stag's Horn Fern is propagated from spores in nurseries. Adventitious shoots bearing daughter plants occasionally arise on the roots. These can be detached and grown in a glass or plastic case at a temperature of 24−26 °C (75−79 °F) with maximum air humidity. Mature plants are grown in rooms with diffused light at a temperature of 15−18 °C (59−64 °F) with extra air humidity provided, even during the winter.

Plants should be repotted between March and June in a porous, well aerated mixture of half-decomposed leafmould, fibrous peat and sphagnum moss at a pH of 4.5−5.5.

Liberal watering and frequent misting of the foliage is desirable in summer, but during the winter watering should be cautious, though in flats where the air is dry the fronds should be gently misted over every now and then. Feed the plants from March to November with a solution of compound fertiliser.

3

P. hillii does not grow as large and is more often found in cultivation. The Regal Elk-horn Fern, *P. grande* (3), is a robust plant with large sterile fronds up to 50 cm (20 in) in diameter, and grows 2 metres (6½ ft) across. This fern is best grown in large greenhouses at a winter temperature of about 20 °C (68 °F).

Stag's Horn Ferns make quite long-lasting house plants, provided they are given careful treatment. They do best in tropical cases and heated winter gardens and are suitable for decorating large epiphytic trunks and branches as well. They should always be grown in slight shade.

1

2

Primula, Primrose
Primula obconica

Primulaceae

The Primula genus includes several hundred distinct species. Primroses are most widely distributed in China, where they do best at about 500 m (1,600 ft) above sea level. A considerable difference between average winter and summer temperatures and variable rainfall are characteristic of the climate there. Mean winter temperatures fall to 6 °C (43 °F), occasionally even below freezing, while in summer the temperature rises to 26−28 °C (79−82 °F). There is little rain in December and January, but in July and August there is usually about 200 mm (8 in), though no dry season follows. The atmosphere is rather humid throughout the year.

Primulas should therefore be grown at low temperatures during the winter, as they can stand even −2 °C (28 °F) at times. Watering should almost cease at that time. On the other hand, summer temperatures can be rather high and water can then be given regularly in ample doses. Such conditions can only be provided in greenhouses, so it is recommended to treat primulas as seasonal indoor plants.

P. obconica (1) is a typical gift plant usually in bloom from September to May. Its flowers can be blue-purple, red, pink or white.

Primroses are propagated exclusively from seed in nurseries. They will last longer indoors if kept in slight shade at a temperature of 8−12 °C (46−54 °F).

2

The Fairy or Baby Primrose, *P. malacoides* (2), and *P. sinensis* flower during the winter and in early spring. The Fairy Primrose should be stood as close to a window as possible and watered regularly. Its flowers will last longer if it is kept at a temperature of 5−10 °C (41−50 °F) and the air humidity increased.

P. sinensis (3) needs more careful watering, as an excess of water can rot the plant's crown.

It should be borne in mind that the tiny hairs on the leaf surface of *P. obconica* contain an alkaloid known as primine, which causes an irritating skin allergy in some people who come in contact with it.

1

3

Pteris, Ribbon Fern, Variegated Table Fern
Polypodiaceae

Pteris cretica 'Albo-lineata'

The green-fronded *P. cretica* grows in the humid primeval forests of the subtropics and tropics of all parts of the world. Its cultivation for over a century has yielded a variety of forms and cultivars. The fronds are much divided into long narrow leaflets of various shapes and colours, as in the cultivar 'Albo-lineata' (1).

The indispensable conditions for long-term cultivation of Pteris indoors are high atmospheric moisture and winter temperatures ranging from 10 − 18 °C (50 − 64 °F). High winter temperatures and dry air cause wilting, yellowing and dropping of the fronds. This is probably the reason for this handsome fern being less widely grown now than it used to be.

In indoor conditions, pteris are propagated by division between March and May. Variegated cultivars should be grown in semi-shade or diffused light at a temperature of 15 − 18 °C (59 − 64 °F). Regular liberal watering as well as frequent misting of the foliage are recommended during the summer. In winter, water should be given sparingly, though the compost should not be allowed to dry out. Repotting should be done from April to June in a mixture of 2 parts coarse leafmould and 1 part loam plus 1 part of peat at a pH of 5.0 − 6.0. From April to August, plants should also be fed with a solution of compound fertiliser.

As pteris have a limited life in rooms where the air is dry, they can only be grown successfully in closed plant cases or flower windows or in humid winter gardens, generally forming an underplanting for other plants.

The following variegated species and cultivars are found in cultivation:
P. cretica 'Alexandrae', 'Victoriae',
P. quadriaurita 'Argyrea' (2) as well as the Sword Brake, *P. ensiformis,* and its cultivars 'Victoriae', and 'Evergemiensis'. *Pteris cretica* 'Wimsettii' bears deeply dissected and clustered leaves.

The Cliff Brake or Button Fern, *Pellaea rotundifolia,* is a small fern of pendulous habit with stiff glossy leaves. It doesn't demand high winter temperatures. This is a suitable fern for hanging baskets.

2

1

185

Indian Azalea
Ericaceae

Rhododendron simsii 'Vervaeneana'

Rhododendron breeding has yielded a good many cultivars since the beginning of last century. Indian Azaleas, including *R. simsii* 'Vervaeneana' (1), are particularly important as house plants.

Flowering azaleas need plenty of water. Bought plants should be watered regularly with soft water so the root ball is well-moistened. Excess water should not be poured out of the dish. Given these conditions, a full display of flowers is assured, even in rooms at a temperature of 18 − 20 °C (64 − 68 °F). The optimum temperature for long-term cultivation is much lower, ranging from 6 − 10 °C (43 − 50 °F), temperatures to be found in unheated corridors, halls, on verandas and in flower windows.

After flowering an azalea should be potted on to the next sized pot filled with a porous compost, prepared by mixing 1 part pulverised bark and 1 part fibrous peat at a pH of 4.0 − 4.5. Pinch shoots back to about five leaves to form a dome shaped plant.

From May onwards, azaleas should be grown in a light airy position preferably plunged in soil in the garden, or on a balcony. Throughout this time, plants should be watered almost daily and sprayed with water on sunny days. Extra feeding is desirable at weekly intervals from May to July, preferably with a compound fertiliser high in nitrogen. In September azaleas should be brought back into a cool room but from February onwards they can again be exposed to higher temperatures of 15 − 18 °C (59 − 64 °F).

1

Specialised nurseries propagate these azaleas vegetatively. The plants are offered for sale from December to May. Early-flowering cultivars like 'Eri Schäme' (2) are more demanding in their requirements than cultivars that flower from February to May. These include, for example, 'Elsa Karger' (3) and 'Leopold Astrid' (4). In the home azaleas can be placed close to a window or in semi-shade. They will stand direct sunlight, though the compost is apt to dry out more rapidly when the plant is exposed to sun.

Boat Lily
Rhoeo spathacea 'Vittata'
(syn. *R. discolor*)

Commelinaceae

The only plant of its genus, *Rhoeo spathacea* comes from Central America and Mexico. Its long lanceolate leaves with longitudinal light stripes are green above and dark violet beneath and borne in rosettes on a short stem. The whole plant grows about 40 cm (16 in) high. The cultivar 'Vittata' (1) has more attractively coloured leaves but the same habit of growth as the species itself. The plant flowers irregularly, bearing tiny white flowers hidden among the leaves.

In nurseries, the Boat Lily is propagated from seed, but in amateur conditions, propagation is done by detaching shoots with two or three fully developed leaves and basal roots. The shoots root in a mixture of peat and sand at a temperature of 18−20 °C (64−68 °F) and high air humidity. During the winter, adult plants should be placed in a light position and grown at a temperature of 16−20 °C (61−68 °F). Watering should be regular in summer but less frequent during the winter. Keep up a high air humidity at temperatures above 18 °C (64 °F).

Between April and August, plants should be repotted in a mixture of 2 parts leafmould, 1 part loam and ½ part sand at a pH of 5.5−6.5. A solution of compound fertiliser should be given during the same period. The boat lily can be grown in flower windows and plant cases. The foliage will turn yellow and drop in dry air or draughts.

2

Setcreasea purpurea (syn. *S. pallida*) (2) belongs to the same family. This semi-erect herbaceous plant comes from the tropics of Mexico. Its prominently jointed shoots are swollen at the nodes. The leaves are long, lanceolate and clasp the stem at the base. The whole plant is a deep purple colour.

Setcreaseas can be planted in bowls and hanging containers, which should be stood in a fairly warm humid

1

environment or in flower windows. This
plant will not tolerate waterlogged or
dried out compost but needs frequent
misting on warm days. Leafy shoots can
be cut and added to flower bouquets in
vases or used in kenzan arrangements.
This plant has been shown to grow
successfully in a hydroponic solution.

189

Saintpaulia, African Violet
Saintpaulia ionantha

Gesneriaceae

The species *S. ionantha* and *S. confusa,* which originated in the East-African tropical forests, provided the basic breeding material from which dozens of cultivars have been developed. In Europe, hybrids of *S. ionantha* (1) have become the most widespread. Their leaves are regularly arranged, the flowers are produced evenly and the plants are generally less fastidious about cultivation conditions. The flowers are mostly blue, violet and pink. The petals may have smooth margins or be attractively waved (2, 3, 4).

Saintpaulias are propagated from leaf cuttings between January and August. The leaf stalks should be cut back to leave only 1−2 cm (½−¾ in), then inserted close together in pans filled with a mixture of equal parts peat and sand. They root in deep shade at a soil temperature of 18−20 °C (64−68 °F) and an air temperature of 22−25 °C (72−77 °F). The highest possible air humidity is recommended. After about two months, the young plants should be potted in 7 cm (3 in) pots, then when they have become potbound, they should be moved on into 10 cm (4 in) pots.

Mature plants need slight shade, a steady temperature of 18−22 °C (64−72 °F) and a room where the air is extra humid. Water which has been left to stand overnight should be poured into a dish to water them from the bottom, as saintpaulias dislike their compost being soaked. An excessively damp atmosphere encourages the development of fungal diseases. Plants that have finished flowering should be repotted when potbound in a light mixture of 1 part leafmould, 1 part peat and ½ part sand at a pH 5.5−6.5. Every two weeks from February to October, the plants should be fed with a solution of compound fertiliser.

3

4

Saintpaulias make quite long-lived plants for the home, bearing flowers regularly for several years if suitable conditions are provided for them. They should be protected from direct sunlight, which can damage their leaves. African violets are usually grown singly in pots as specimen plants.

Well-developed specimens can be propagated by dividing the clumps. Plants obtained in this way start flowering sooner than those propagated from leaf cuttings.

Saintpaulias are among the few flowering plants which do well in soilless compost.

1

2

Sansevieria, Mother-in-law's Tongue, Bowstring Hemp

Liliaceae

Sansevieria trifasciata 'Laurentii'

Sansevierias are among the most highly valued indoor plants, as they are exceptionally tough and long-lived and adapt well to most kinds of environment, besides being resistant to diseases. *Sansevieria trifasciata* 'Laurentii' (1) from South Africa is a particularly good plant for indoor cultivation. Its erect tufts of flat sword-like concave leaves spring from a fleshy underground rhizome. The leaves are cross-banded in a silvery colour and the margins are longitudinally striped with yellow. The leaves reach up to 50 — 120 cm (20 — 47 in) high and measure 4 — 8 cm (1½ — 3 in) wide. Mature plants produce a cluster of fragrant greenish-white flowers.

Adequate light has a benefical effect on the leaf colouring, but plants that have not become accustomed to it can be harmed by direct sunlight. Sansevierias can even be grown in deep shade or in artificial light. The plant's only reaction to extreme shortage of light is to develop narrower leaves. Plants tolerate temperatures above 20 °C (68 °F) and dry air in centrally-heated homes. The optimum winter temperature is 16 — 18 °C (61 — 64 °F) though plants will survive undamaged if there is a temporary fall in temperature to 12 — 14 °C (54 — 59 °F), provided they are kept almost dry. Sansevierias are very sensitive to the amount of water in their compost. They seem to stand an occasional shortage of water better than long-term overwatering, which can set up a bacterial disease of the crown of the plant and the bases of the leaves. Too high an air humidity can also cause leaf rot, so the plants should not be syringed during the summer. A porous compost, such as a mixture of 3 parts peat and 1 part loam at a pH of about 6.0 has proved suitable.

2

The plants need feeding from March to the end of September with a solution of compound fertiliser high in potash.

The following cultivars are also grown as indoor plants: *S. trifasciata* 'Hahnii' (2) with leaves arranged in a low, broad rosette, 'Golden Hahnii', which looks very similar but has broad yellow bands, and 'Silver Hahnii' with shining silvery leaves. As these cultivars grow only about 20 — 30 cm (8 — 12 in) high they are particularly good plants for small rooms. The cultivar 'Gigantea' (3) grows 40—50 cm (15—20 in) high.

All sansevierias are quite easily propagated from leaf cuttings. New leaves are only produced by the green-coloured parts of the yellow-banded cultivars, so young plants from cuttings do not reproduce the yellow colouring. This is probably caused by an absence of adventitious buds in the yellow stripes on the leaves. This is why the valuable varieties of sansevierias are propagated by dividing the clumps, each division consisting of several leaves and part of the fleshy rhizome.

193

Cineraria
Senecio cruentus hybrids

Compositae

The cinerarias grown so widely nowadays have very little in common with the wild species, *S. cruentus,* which comes from the Canary Islands. Cineraria breeding is designed to produce early-flowering cultivars with a more compact habit of growth and smaller leaves.

Cinerarias (1) are propagated from seed, usually in nurseries. Their blooms vary in colour from white through pink and blue to violet (2, 3). The plants are offered for sale from March to May. They serve a single purpose, being considered typical spring gift plants. To ensure the maximum crop of blooms and the longest possible flowering period, the indoor gardener should give the plants a position that provides as nearly as possible the conditions the plant is used to in its natural habitat. There cinerarias grow at higher altitudes in relatively low temperatures and high air humidity. They should therefore be given a position in full light or partial shade with the lowest possible temperature (optimum 6—9 °C (43—48 °F)). Plenty of fresh, humid air is absolutely essential.

Cinerarias should be well watered as they dislike dried-out compost. If the soil is allowed to dry out, the plants rapidly wilt and the buds will not open properly. In dry conditions aphids often infest the undersides of the leaves.

2

3

Cinerarias cannot be grown satisfactorily in homes where the average room temperature is 18—20 °C (64—68 °F). They are suitable for decorating halls that are either unheated or whose temperature can be controlled, as well as verandas and staircases. They are often used for spring time decoration of graves or grouped in pottery bowls, which can be placed on balconies or terraces or even in the garden.

In the past, cinerarias were among the most widely cultivated and best-selling house plants, but their use is now rather limited.

1

Gloxinia
Sinningia speciosa hybrids

Gesneriaceae

Nurseries now produce only gloxinias derived from crossing the two species *S. speciosa* and *S. regina* (1). The original species formed part of the herbaceous undergrowth of the primeval tropical forests of Southern Brazil. Gloxinias grown in greenhouses bear single (2), semi-double or double (3) flowers from April to September, depending on when they were sown. Their flowers are usually red, but cultivars bearing blue, pink or white flowers are often seen in cultivation.

Gloxinias are used for seasonal decoration in the summer. They can be harmed by draughts and fluctuating temperatures. In the home they should be placed in diffused light and protected from direct sun, which can cause rapid deterioration in their leaves. To ensure the maximum number of blooms and the longest possible flowering period, gloxinias should be watered regularly and freely with water that has been left to stand overnight. Also provide maximum air humidity. The compost should never be allowed to dry out, so the pot should be placed in a dish which is filled with moist gravel. Water so that the whole of the plant's root ball is moistened. Gloxinias should be misted in the morning on hot sunny days. Faded flowers should be picked off. The plants should only be fed if the gardener wants to keep the tubers for the following year.

2

Gloxinias form underground tubers, which serve as food storage organs. If the gardener decides to grow a Gloxinia from the tuber again the next year, the plant should be fed with a solution of compound fertiliser at least twice during the flowering season to keep the period of vegetative growth going as long as possible. All spent flowers should be nipped off immediately. From September onwards, the plants should be dried off. The tubers should be stored in their pots in a dry room at a temperature of 10−12 °C (50−54 °F). In February the tubers should be lifted, cleaned and planted in pots about 12 cm (5 in) in diameter, depending on the size of the tuber. Fill the pots with a mixture of equal parts leafmould and peat. To

start with the planted tubers should be watered cautiously, but once the leaves have sprouted, watering can gradually become regular and more frequent. Plants can open their flowers as early as the first half of April.

3

1

Christmas Cherry, Solanum
Solanum pseudocapsicum

Solanaceae

Various species of Solanum are scattered in different climatic zones on all continents. But only low-growing, sub-shrubby species are suitable for indoor culture. They bear long-lasting round yellow or orange fruits from October onwards.

S. pseudocapsicum (1), possibly a native of Madeira, has been in cultivation for a long time. It reaches a height of 35–100 cm (13½–39 in). As soon as its small white flowers (2) are over, the fruits containing easily sprouted seeds (3) begin to ripen. Besides being raised from seed, Christmas cherries can be propagated from tip or stem cuttings in February or March. The seeds should be sown in pans filled with a light mixture of loam and sand placed in a greenhouse or covered with glass and grown at a temperature of 16–18 °C (61–64 °F). The seedlings should be pricked out in trays, then later potted in 8–9 cm (3–3½ in) pots. The pots should be plunged in the soil, preferably in a frame or in a slightly shaded garden bed.

While they are growing, the plants should be fed with a solution of compound fertiliser containing extra potash and phosphate. In August the plants should be repotted in 10–12 cm (4–5½ in) pots filled with John Innes potting compost No. 2 at pH 6.0–6.5. Regular watering is desirable during the summer, though if the soil is permanently soaked with water the roots will rot. Before autumn frosts begin the pots should be moved into a well-ventilated room at a temperature of 10–15 °C (50–59 °F).

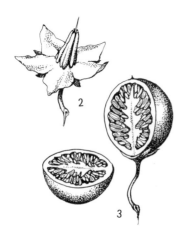

Solanum pseudocapsicum 'New Patterson' bears larger, orange-red fruits. It has a horizontal branching habit and particularly long-lasting fruits.

Christmas cherries are suitable for the autumn and winter decoration of moderately warm rooms, windows and verandas, as well as moderately heated winter gardens. But in too low a temperature the leaves will rot and drop off. In a dry atmosphere the plants can be infested by aphids or less often by whitefly.

1

Spathiphyllum, White Sail, Peace Lily
Spathiphyllum wallisii

Araceae

The various species of Spathiphyllum originate for the most part in the perpetually damp rain forests of Tropical America, where they grow in the shade or semi-shade, forming the undergrowth.

S. wallisii (1) is the most commonly cultivated species. This plant is about 30−40 cm (12−16 in) high and forms many underground suckers. The glossy leaves are dark green, the spathe is pure white and the fragrant spadix is white and yellowish-white.

The plant is propagated by dividing the clumps between February and October, less often from seed. Sections root well in a mixture of leafmould and peat at a soil temperature of 22−24 °C (72−75 °F) and an air temperature 2 °C (4 °F) lower. These young plants should either be misted frequently, or covered with plastic sheeting.

Adult plants are grown at a winter temperature of 18−22 °C (64−72 °F). They are not harmed by a temporary drop in temperature below 15 °C (59 °F), provided the air humidity is reduced and watering is limited at the time. In spring and summer the plants should be grown in semi-shade, but during the winter they should be given more light. Regular, liberal watering is desirable from February to October, but from November to January, smaller doses of water are required. Keep a humid atmosphere throughout the year. Spathiphyllums should be repotted between March and August in a mixture of 2 parts leafmould, 1 part peat and ½ part sand at a pH of 5.0−6.0. Feeding is best done from April to October with a solution of compound fertiliser.

The range of uses for Spathiphyllum as a pot plant is controlled by its demands for humid air and a steady temperature.

Spathiphyllums are therefore suitable for growing in glass plant cases, closed flower windows and greenhouses. This plant doesn't usually thrive in centrally-heated homes, where better results can be gained by growing them in a soilless medium. Spathiphyllum is also occasionally used as a cut flower.

The species *S. blandum* (2) has similar requirements and range of uses as *S. wallisii.*

2

1

Stephanotis, Madagascar Jasmine, Wax Flower
Asclepiadaceae

Stephanotis floribunda

S. floribunda (1) is a native of Madagascar. This climbing plant's woody stems grow up to 3—5 m (10—16 ft) long in favourable conditions. They bear dark green, glossy leathery leaves and intensely fragrant trumpet-shaped, white flowers (2).

The plants are propagated from well-ripened stem cuttings with one pair of leaves. They should be inserted in three to a 7 cm (3 in) pot filled with a mixture of 3 parts peat and 1 part sand. Cuttings root when covered with plastic sheeting or a pane of glass, at a soil temperature of 25—30 °C (77—86 °F). The most favourable conditions for propagation occur from January to April. Rooted plants should be repotted in a larger pot filled with a mixture of 2 parts leafmould, 1 part loam and 1/2 part sand at a pH of 5.5—6.5. Older plants should be repotted in the same mixture between March and May.

Stephanotis should be grown in rooms at a daytime temperature of 16—20 °C (61—68 °F) falling to 12—14 °C (54—57 °F) at night. The lightest possible position will suit them, though they should be protected from the hottest sun. They need plenty of fresh air and a humid atmosphere. From November to February, water should be given cautiously at longish intervals, but during the active growing season watering should be liberal. Every two weeks from March to August, plants should also be fed with a solution of compound fertiliser low in nitrogen. At high temperatures aphids often infest the leaves and flowers.

2

During its growing season, the shoots should be pinched back and tied to wooden or metal supports. A full crop of flowers is only produced when the correct temperatures are provided and watering is not overdone. Lower air humidity in winter and sufficient light are also essential. Well-ripened shoots flower best.

The plant's need for a wide range between day and night temperatures limits its range of uses. Stephanotis doesn't usually thrive in centrally-heated rooms, but does better in winter gardens where the temperature can be controlled, on verandas and in moderately heated halls with extra air humidity.

1

Strelitzia, Bird of Paradise Flower
Strelitzia reginae

Musaceae

Strelitzias are prolific plants native to the South African rain forests. One of the most commonly found species, *S. reginae* (1), reaches a height of about 2 m (6 ft 6 in) and width of 150 cm (5 ft) when mature. Its leathery grey-green leaves with long stems spring up in clusters from the underground stem. The roots are robust and fleshy. Older plants spread by underground suckers, from which new plants develop.

Vigorous young plants suitable for growing on can be obtained by detaching the young plants in February or March, or when the flowers have finished. To succeed at this it is essential to let the lateral suckers develop their own strong roots before the plant is divided. The cut surfaces should be dusted with charcoal powder and left to dry. At the same time of year mature strelitzias should be repotted, usually once in every two or three years. The most suitable compost for repotting is a medium heavy mixture rich in nutrients, such as 1 part soil-based potting compost and ½ part sand at a pH of 6.0—6.5.

From March to October, a solution of compound fertiliser should be given regularly at weekly intervals. Liberal watering is necessary from the end of February to October, for strelitzias consume a lot of water during this period. On hot days, the foliage should be sprayed with water too. Strelitzias don't mind summer temperatures above 30 °C (86 °F), but in winter they should be kept almost dry at temperatures ranging from 8 to 12 °C (46—54 °F).

2

In Europe, strelitzias do not make typical pot plants, due to their size and vigour, but are grown mainly for their cut flowers. But their exotic orange and blue flowers are so attractive to plant-lovers that there have been repeated attempts to grow strelitzias outside greenhouses, for instance on spacious glassed-in verandas and in light positions in winter gardens. They are planted in deep containers or straight into the open soil. The layer of soil should be at least 50 cm (20 in) deep. The cut flowers will last in a vase for 4—6 weeks.

The cultivar 'Humilis' (2) reaches a height of about 1 m (3 ft 3 in), and has broader, dark green leaves. It is suitable for growing as a pot plant.

1

Cape Primrose
Streptocarpus hybrids

Gesneriaceae

The mountain rain forests of South-East Africa and Madagascar are home to several dozen species of Streptocarpus. Most are terrestrial, growing in light soil rich in humus, but some are epiphytes. Large-scale efforts to cross selected species began as early as the beginning of last century. Consequently the plants which are grown and offered for sale nowadays are exclusively of hybrid origin (1). Their appearance reminds many people of gloxinias, bearing a smaller number of tongue-like lanceolate leaves, narrower than a gloxinia's. The flowers are more numerous, in a range of clear, bright colours. Each slender flower stem bears a single bloom or a cluster of flowers, which can be blue, violet, red, pink or white (2, 3, 4).

The plants are propagated from seed in nurseries. Flowering plants are offered for sale from April to June or in August, according to the time of sowing. Young plants can also be raised from leaf cuttings. They are suitable for decorating cool, rather humid rooms with generous ventilation.

During the summer, Cape Primroses do well in partial shade at a temperature of 18−20 °C (64−68 °F). Frequent watering is desirable throughout their growing season, as the plants should be grown in small (9−10 cm/3½−4 in) pots, so the compost can dry out more rapidly. Extra air humidity is provided by misting the foliage frequently and allowing water to evaporate from the gravel tray in which the pot is standing. At flowering time, Cape Primroses can be given two or three feeds of compound fertiliser high in phosphates and potash. Spent flowers should be promptly nipped off.

When the flowers are over, the plants should be grown in a temperature of 10−15 °C (50−59 °F) and watered sparingly. These conditions encourage the plant to become almost dormant for a while. In February the plants should be potted on into larger pots filled with a mixture of 2 parts leafmould, 1 part peat, 1 part loam and ½ part sand at a pH of 5.5.−6.5. Fresh growth is encouraged by regular watering and increasing the temperature to 16−18 °C (61−64 °F).

Cape Primroses bloom for a second time in April, even more prolifically than in late summer. When the plants have finished flowering, they should be kept on

the dry side so that they take rest. The
shrivelled leaves should be removed. In
the following years Cape Primroses can
be increased by division.

2

1

207

Succulents

Besides the succulent cacti (members of the Cactaceae), there are many succulents belonging to the Crassulaceae, Liliaceae, Agavaceae, Euphorbiaceae and other families. Africa, Central and South America, the Canary Islands and Madagascar are the main areas of their natural distribution. These plants overcome the adverse climatic conditions by conserving large amounts of water in the storage tissues of their fleshy stems and then gradually using it during periods of shortage.

It is difficult to choose a few typical representatives from the vast number of succulents, as plants from different families and genera differ not only in appearance, but in their individual cultural requirements. Among the popular succulents are, for example, the cultivars produced by crossing *Kalanchoe blossfeldiana* (1) of the family Crassulaceae with other species of Kalanchoe. They do well even in dry homes at a winter temperature of 15—18 °C (59—64 °F). They should be placed in a light position. Slight shade is only required by young plants that are still rooting and by adult plants scorched by hot sun. Repotting is best done between March and April or at the end of July and in August. A porous gritty soil-based potting compost at a pH of 5.5—6.5 is the most suitable growing medium.

Watering should be done carefully, particularly during the winter, as an excess of water in the soil can start to rot the base of the stem. During their growing season, the plants should be fed with fortnightly doses of compound fertiliser.

Crassula arborescens (2), which has long been in cultivation, also belongs to the Crassulaceae family. Plants growing in the wild reach a height of 3 m (10 ft). This Crassula's range of uses is similar to the Kalanchoe's. From the end of November to February, watering should be reduced to a minimum and the plants should be completely rested at a temperature of 8—10 °C (46—50 °F).

Aloe arborescens, a member of the family Liliaceae, is widely grown as a medicinal plant.

The Century Plant, *Agave americana* (3), is used for outdoor decoration in summer. It is a robust plant bearing large spiny-tipped grey leaves with short teeth.

There are cultivars striped in white or
yellow. This plant will come through the
winter at temperatures of 5—10 °C
(41—50 °F).

Succulents are most often grown
together with cacti, either in special
greenhouses, or in flower windows and
glass plant cases.

Syngonium, Goose Foot Plant

Syngonium podophyllum 'Albolineatum'

Araceae

Some 20 species of Syngonium are native to the tropical regions of South and Central America. These climbing plants are attached to the bark of trees by means of their aerial roots. They require the same growing conditions as philodendrons.

At present, the variegated cultivars of *S. podophyllum,* such as 'Albolineatum' (1), 'Green Gold', 'Imperial White' and others are most widely grown. The palmately incised leaves are coloured olive-green, with a distinct yellow, yellowish-white or yellowish-green pattern. They are generally propagated from tip cuttings. Insert several cuttings in a small pot, preferably during the period from February to November. They strike roots quite quickly in a mixture of leafmould or peat and sand, at a temperature of 22—24 °C (72—75 °F). Older plants can be propagated by division as well.

In winter, they should be grown at a room temperature of 18—20 °C (64—68 °F). If the temperature falls below 14 °C (57 °F) for any length of time, the leaves turn yellow and the roots rot. Plants should be placed out of reach of direct sunlight. They will tolerate deep shade, but this results in dull leaf coloration. The amount and frequency of watering depends on the temperature and the size of the plant. Plants thrive in high atmospheric moisture. They should be repotted between March and September in a mixture of 2 parts leafmould and 1 part peat at a pH 5.0—6.5. A solution of compound fertiliser should be given from February to October.

2

Five Fingers, *S. auritum* (2), is another commonly grown species, bearing glossy leaves coloured emerald green. Its demands are similar to those of *S. podophyllum,* except that it is more sensitive to waterlogged compost.

The evergreen syngoniums make very long-lasting house plants. They are quite popular, thanks to their quick growth and easy propagation. They are grown trailing downwards or trained up supports, and tolerate central heating. The leaves tend to dry off during the winter, due to the lower air humidity, but they are quickly replaced by new ones later. Syngoniums also make excellent plants for hydroponics.

1

Tillandsia, Pink Quill
Tillandsia cyanea

Bromeliaceae

Tillandsias are among the smallest bromeliads in cultivation. Their home is South and Central America, where they grow largely as epiphytes.

Tillandsias can be divided into two groups as regards their cultivation. The first group comprises tillandsias that grow in a layer of coarse, half-decomposed humus, generally as a part of the undergrowth or on rocks. The Pink Quill, *T. cyanea* (1), as well as the Blue Flowered Torch, *T. lindenii*, belong to this group. Tillandsias which are attached to the bark of the trees by means of aerial roots, such as *T. ionantha* and many others, form the second group. Plants belonging to the first group are more widely grown by nurseries.

T. cyanea blooms from March to August. It can be propagated by division between June and September, as it is quite quick to form offsets. It cannot be propagated from seed without special facilities. This tillandsia does well in a light position out of reach of direct sunlight, at winter temperatures of 16−20 °C (61−68 °F). Watering and syringing with soft water should be carried out according to the temperature. The plant seems to prefer to dry out occasionally rather than have a permanently waterlogged compost. Keep the atmosphere as humid as possible.

June to September is also the best time for repotting older plants. They thrive in a mixture of equal parts of coarse peat and half-decomposed leafmould with some perlite added (pH 4.5−5.5). They should be fed at fortnightly intervals from February to November with a weak solution of compound fertiliser.

2

Pot-grown tillandsias can be used to decorate large epiphytic trunks and branches in closed flower windows and winter gardens. This applies to *T. flabellata* (2), for example, which bears narrow light green leaves, shining red bracts and blue flowers.

Spanish Moss or Old Man's Beard, *T. usneoides* (3), bears five light grey leaves and small flowers of a greenish yellow colour. It is a pendulous plant forming long clusters of foliage, which

hang on branches or bark in the humid
atmosphere of a plant case, preferably at
temperatures of 18—22 °C (64—72 °F).
Warm greenhouses provide the best
environment for growing tillandsias on
a wider scale.

213

Tradescantia, Wandering Jew, Travelling Sailor
Commelinaceae

Tradescantia albiflora 'Albo-vittata'

The evergreen tradescantias are the most commonly encountered and most modest of house plants. They came originally from the tropics and sub-tropics of America, where some 40 species grow in the wild. Tradescantias are semi-erect or trailing plants, whose shoots can grow several metres long.

A native of Central America, *T. albiflora* is one of the species most often found as a pot plant. Its leaves are green above and pale purple beneath. The leaves of the cultivar 'Albo-vittata' (1) are striped with white. Coloured sap can be squeezed out of the stem or leaves of the species itself, but the sap of the variegated cultivars is clear, as is that of the species *T. fluminensis.*

All tradescantias are easily propagated from stem cuttings throughout the year. They should be planted close together in 10 cm (4 in) pots or bowls, where they quickly root in a mixture of peat and sand. They root best at a temperature of 18−20 °C (64−68 °F) with extra air humidity. Later, the green-leaved species are happy at 6−10 °C (43−50 °F) during the winter, but the variegated ones need a minimum temperature of 12 °C (54 °F). Tradescantias tolerate any kind of indoor light conditions apart from direct sunlight. Keep the compost slightly moist all the time. They do best in a humid environment, though they will also tolerate centrally-heated homes.

Tradescantias should be fed in the growing period at weekly intervals with a solution of compound fertiliser.

2

The Flowering Inch Plant, *T. blossfeldiana,* is another species widely grown as a pot plant. It has olive-green leaves, purple on the undersides.

Zebrina pendula (2), which is also called Wandering Jew, closely resembles the tradescantias. It is a pendulous plant whose leaves are purple on the underside and have two striking silvery bands on the upper side.

Tradescantias are fairly long-lived house plants. They are often used to decorate areas like corridors, staircases and lobbies. They do well when grown hydroponically and also root easily in clear water. Dull leaf coloration in variegated cultivars is likely to be caused by overfeeding with nitrogen or by poor light conditions.

1

Vriesia, Flaming Sword
Vriesia splendens

Bromeliaceae

Most of the bromeliads grow in South and Central America, and these areas are home to all the species of Vriesia found in cultivation. Vriesias are mostly epiphytes, bearing leaves with ornamental stripes, which are arranged in a perfect funnel-like rosette. The spiky inflorescence is attractively coloured.

V. splendens (1) is the most popular species in this genus. Plants with short, well-coloured leaves and a long red or orange-red inflorescence are the most highly valued. The true flowers are yellow.

Propagation from seed is rather difficult if it is attempted anywhere but in a greenhouse. However, if the inflorescence is removed after flowering, the plant will form one to three offsets that develop into young plants, given favourable conditions. When the offsets have grown strong enough, they can be detached and potted in 6−7 cm (2½−2¾ in) pots filled with a porous well-aerated compost prepared from young leafmould, peat, pulverised pine bark and perlite at a pH of 5.0−5.5. They root in high air humidity, at a soil temperature of 22−26 °C (72−79 °F). Rooted cuttings should be grown in diffused light at a temperature of 20−22 °C (68−72 °F). Young and mature plants alike should have water poured into the 'vase' to keep the leaf rosette from drying out. Keep the compost slightly moist as well. Vriesias should also be fed at fortnightly intervals from March to November, preferably with a weak solution of compound fertiliser. The inflorescence will last about two or three months, after which the plant gradually dies off.

3

The Netted Vriesia, *V. fenestralis* (2), is a plant of robust growth, with a leaf rosette that reaches 90 cm (3 ft) in diameter. It is highly ornamental by reason of its broad light green leaves with transverse net pattern. It can be used in large tropical windows, greenhouses and conservatories.

More compact kinds of vriesia, such as *Vriesia × poelmannii* (3), are suitable for decorating flower windows and plant cases, as well as trunks and branches used to display epiphytes. Flowering plants can be used even in centrally-heated homes, where they can be grown hydroponically.

2

1

217

Plants suitable for rooms with low temperatures during the winter, less than 15 °C (59 °F), and an air humidity of more than 50%.

Araucaria heterophylla
Asparagus densiflorus
Aspidistra elatior
Aucuba japonica
Cacti
Campanula isophylla
Chamaerops humilis
Chlorophytum comosum
Citrus reticulata
Clerodendrum thomsonae
Clivia miniata
Coleus blumei hybrids
Euonymus japonicus
Fatshedera lizei
Fatsia japonica
Fuchsia hybrids
Hedera helix

Hibiscus rosa-sinensis
Hydrangea macrophylla
Haemanthus katharinae
Laurus nobilis
Myrtus communis
Nerium oleander
Passiflora caerulea
Pelargonium peltatum hybrids
Pilea cadierei
Primula obconica
Rhododendron simsii
Senecio cruentus hybrids
Solanum pseudocapsicum
Strelitzia reginae
Succulents
Tradescantia albiflora
and *fluminensis*

Plants suitable for rooms where the temperature fluctuates during the winter and that are locally or centrally heated with a maximum temperature of 20 °C (68 °F) during the day and 2−4 °C (4−8 °F) lower at night. Air humidity 40−60%.

Aechmea fasciata
Araucaria heterophylla
Asparagus densiflorus
Aspidistra elatior
Aucuba japonica
Capsicum annuum
Ceropegia woodii
Chamaedorea elegans
Chamaerops humilis
Chlorophytum comosum
Cissus rhombifolia
Clivia miniata
Coleus blumei hybrids
Cyperus alternifolius
Ficus elastica

Fuchsia hybrids
Howea belmoreana
Hoya carnosa
Monstera deliciosa
Nephrolepis exaltata
Philodendron scandens
Phoenix canariensis
Platycerium bifurcatum
Sansevieria trifasciata
Schlumbergera truncata
Stephanotis floribunda
Streptocarpus hybrids
Syngonium podophyllum
Tradescantia albiflora
and *fluminensis*

Plants suitable for centrally-heated rooms with a constant temperature of 18−22 °C (64−72 °F) and an air humidity of 30−50%.

Aechmea fasciata
Aglaonema commutatum
Anthurium scherzerianum hybrids
Brassaia actinophylla
Chamaedorea elegans
Cissus rhombifolia
Clivia miniata
Codiaeum variegatum (some of the cultivars)
Cryptanthus zonatus
Dieffenbachia picta (some of the cultivars)
Dracaena deremensis
Epipremnum aureum
Ficus elastica

Guzmania minor (while in flower)
Howea belmoreana
Monstera deliciosa
Neoregelia carolinae (flowering plants only)
Pandanus veitchii (with extra air humidity)
Philodendron scandens
Phoenix canariensis
Saintpaulia ionantha
Sansevieria trifasciata
Syngonium podophyllum
Tradescantia albiflora and fluminensis
Vriesia splendens

Plants suitable for enclosed spaces with a controlled atmosphere — flower windows, glass plant cases, winter gardens and greenhouses.

Aeschynanthus marmoratus
Ananas comosus
Anthurium scherzerianum hybrids
Aphelandra squarrosa
Asplenium nidus
Brunfelsia pauciflora
Caladium bicolor
Calathea makoyana
Codiaeum variegatum
Columnea gloriosa
Cordyline terminalis
Dieffenbachia picta (some of the cultivars)
Dizygotheca elegantissima

Fittonia verschaffeltii
Guzmania minor
Maranta leuconeura
Neoregelia carolinae
Paphiopedilum hybrids
Pachystachys lutea
Peperomia obtusifolia
Pilea cadierei
Platycerium bifurcatum
Pteris cretica
Rhoeo spathacea
Spathiphyllum wallisii
Tillandsia cyanea
Vriesia splendens

INDEX
Page numbers in italics indicate illustrations

222